When The ~~Right~~ Wrong One Comes

Identifying The Wrong One

By Greg Davis

LEEDS
PUBLISHING HOUSE

ISBN 979-8-89660-061-9

This information is given to us to understand that the author is engaged in rendering legal or professional advice. The opinions expressed by the author are not necessarily those of LEEDS PRESS CORP.

Table of Contents

INTRODUCTION

In this book, I offer more than mere words; I provide a guiding light—a beacon of wisdom from years of observing, learning, and understanding the complex changing aspects of relationships. This book is a comprehensive guide to discerning the hidden indicators and the not-so-hidden red flags that separate a worthy partner from the one you should walk away from. As a seasoned witness who has seen the evolving nature of romantic engagements, I feel a profound responsibility to impart my gathered knowledge to you, the reader, who may find yourself at a junction of hope and desperation.

My goal here is straightforward and bold: to arm you with wisdom on keeping your heart safe while staying open to love. In today's fast-moving world, finding love can feel like walking through a maze, with each step holding the thrill of connection or the pain of heartbreak. But it's in these uncertain moments that we learn the most. Through this book, I'll walk with you, pointing out the red flags, showing you the signs we often ignore, and helping you read the intentions of those who come into your life.

Looking back, I've noticed two common mistakes: moving too fast and making poor choices. These go hand in hand. Rushing into relationships usually comes from loneliness, a feeling that can make anyone's presence feel like **"the one"**. Society pressures us, especially women, to settle down or start families by a certain age, which can push people into commitments before truly knowing the other person.

This pressure creates a ticking clock, leading to quick decisions without seeing how someone handles loss, stress, or just life's ups and downs. Missing these signs can mean getting into a relationship that can't stand life's tests. It's not that the person is necessarily "bad," but they may not be right for you. Learning to see these mismatches early on means understanding what you need and being firm about your boundaries. This book highlights why it's crucial not to compromise on what matters most to you in a relationship; otherwise, you risk staying with someone you already know deep down isn't right for you.

Prevention, empowerment, and building healthy, respectful relationships are at the heart of this journey. You need to heal and be whole to attract the right partner. Making choices from a place of strength, not weakness, is key. This book is here to guide you—not just to find the right person, but to be the right person. With each chapter, let the lessons sharpen your intuition and strengthen your spirit. This way, you'll see those who aren't for you, not with bitterness, but with the quiet confidence of someone who knows their worth and path.

CHAPTER 1

They Distract You from You

In this chapter, we dig into how toxic relationships can make you forget about the most important person in your life – yourself. When things aren't going well with a partner, it's too easy to stop looking out for your goals and well-being. You might find yourself bending over backward just to keep them happy, and before you know it, you've put yourself on the back burner. This kind of self-neglect can slowly take away from who you are. Here, we talk about why it's essential to stay true to yourself and keep growing as a person, no matter your relationship. By understanding how a relationship can affect how you see and treat yourself, you can make better choices that honor your needs and who you are.

When a partner starts pulling you away from focusing on yourself, it can show up in ways that range from loud and clear to quietly sneaky. One common tactic is demanding constant communication – wanting updates, texts, or calls all day. This can drain your encrgy, leaving you no time for the things that interest you or just for quiet time.

Another way they might keep you distracted is by creating a sense of dependency. They may start encouraging or manipulating you to rely on them for emotional support, decision-making, finances, or even your social life. This can chip away at your independence and confidence. At the same time, they might criticize things you care about, like your hobbies, job, or friends. They might laugh at your interests or show zero interest, making you lose excitement for your passions. Over time, you might even give up these things to keep the peace or win their approval.

Partners can also cross the line by disrespecting your personal boundaries. They might ignore or push back against the limits you set around your own space, your alone time, or the things you enjoy doing solo. This makes it challenging to stay balanced, keeping you from having a healthy mix between being yourself and being with them. Plus, they might use emotional manipulation—making you feel guilty or ashamed or even pulling away their affection as a way to control your choices. This can make you feel like you're being selfish just for wanting to focus on your own growth or putting yourself first for a change.

Some partners might try to fill up all your time with plans, packing the schedule with things to do together without even asking you. Or they'll insist on joining events you used to enjoy on your own or with others. This cuts down on your time to just think, unwind, or care for yourself, and it slowly pushes you to the edge, limiting your freedom to just be. They might also pick away your confidence by commenting negatively about your looks, intelligence, or abilities. This sort of talk can slowly chip away at your self-esteem, making you feel like their approval is what matters most.

A partner might even go as far as to isolate you from your support networks. They'll discourage you from staying close to family and friends or find ways to stir up conflicts with them, cutting you off from the people who've got your back. Another profound tactic is gaslighting, where they make you question your own experiences or sanity by denying things that happened, twisting the facts, or lying about the past. This manipulation can make you doubt yourself sincerely, leaving you feeling lost and putting their needs and views above your own.

Recognizing these behaviors is crucial if you're going to address them and refocus on your growth and self-care. By staying aware of how these patterns play out in a relationship, you can make moves to protect your individuality and ensure your needs are met. This awareness is key to looking after your well-being and building healthier, more balanced connections.

Toxicity in a relationship is like a slow-acting poison—sneaky, spreading, and deeply harmful. It creates an environment that, if left unchecked, can turn even the best of people into sources of negativity. It's like a venomous bite, leaving wounds that keep festering, and it's critical to spot the warning signs before this toxicity seeps in and spreads.

One tell-tale sign of a toxic partner is the uncertainty they bring into the relationship. You might find yourself constantly guessing where you stand with them. They're fully committed one moment, then acting distant and unsure the next. This keeps you on an emotional rollercoaster, where they control every twist and turn, leaving you feeling unsteady and emotionally drained.

Another red flag is their unpredictable behavior. With a toxic partner, you're walking on eggshells because you never know what mood they'll be in. They can swing from showing intense affection to treating you with cold indifference, all without warning. These constant shifts take a toll, leaving you mentally exhausted.

You might also notice that their affection comes and goes like a flickering light. They'll shower you with attention and make you feel on top of the world, only to pull back and go cold without apparent reason. This push-and-pull leaves you feeling confused and shut out as they withdraw into themselves, cutting off the connection just when you need it most.

Toxic partners often struggle with communication, shifting between being fully engaged and then totally checked out. They get so caught up in their feelings that they neglect yours, making it challenging to maintain a stable and supportive connection.

Toxicity also has a way of spreading. The longer you stay around a toxic person, the more you risk picking up their habits, creating a cycle of negative behavior that you might unknowingly pass on to others. This can lead to a chain of emotional harm that goes beyond just you and your partner.

The harm done by toxic relationships often goes way deeper than the fights you can see. It leaves scars—depression, regret, sometimes even post-traumatic stress. Over time, you might even pull away from relationships altogether, feeling unworthy or rejected. Spotting these signs is crucial, not just for your immediate happiness but for your long-term emotional health. Toxicity is like poison, but it's also like toxic waste. Toxic partners dump their emotional baggage on you, their unresolved issues, their past hurts, and all that negativity. This stuff is dangerous to your mental and emotional health, and sometimes a relationship filled with this level of toxicity just isn't safe to be in.

A major warning sign of a toxic partner is the constant feeling of uncertainty they create. Another big one is how they handle conflict. Instead of addressing issues directly, they might spread your private business everywhere—friends, family, even social media. When they make your problems public, it's like they're avoiding real conversation. If they can't say it to your face, they shouldn't be saying it at all. A toxic partner doesn't respect the privacy of your relationship, and that's a huge red flag.

Five Signs Your Partner Is Toxic

1. **They constantly leave you feeling uncertain about the relationship.** One day, they like you; the next day, they're unsure, leaving you wondering where you stand.

2. **When things aren't going well, they talk about your business to anyone who will listen.** They trash you to their friends, their family, even their mom—airing all your personal problems to the world.

3. **They use social media to send you indirect, subliminal messages because they're too cowardly to address issues face-to-face.** Instead of communicating with you, they post vague, petty comments that you know are about you. It's a low, petty way to handle conflict and hurt.

4. **Toxic partners often know they're toxic, but they won't admit it.** They bring out the worst in you, and before you know it, you start acting in ways that aren't true to who you are. This is why being with a toxic person isn't healthy, it changes you for the worse.

5. **If you're in this kind of relationship, the best thing to do is tell them to "go with God," bless them and let them go.** It's important to recognize these signs before you lose yourself trying to deal with someone who won't

change. Toxic people bring out more toxicity in you, and that's not the place you ever want to go.

You can't help a toxic person until they recognize it themselves. They need to wake up and admit, "I'm toxic." A toxic person makes everything about themselves, leaving no room for you. Some of you are in toxic relationships, and honestly, no matter what it takes, you need to get out.

But this isn't just about spotting if your partner is toxic; it's also about recognizing if you might be, too. Sometimes, it's necessary to take a step back and do a self-check. Every lesson I share here is one I've had to learn myself—I'm speaking from experience. You might be with someone who brings out the toxicity in you because, let's face it, we all have a bit of it. The wrong person will drag it out, and if you don't deal with it, you'll carry it right into the next relationship.

In psychology, "toxicity" in a relationship is about patterns of behavior that continuously chip away at one or both partners' well-being. These behaviors can be emotional, psychological, or even physical. They create an environment that's harmful, taking a toll on the emotional health and safety of everyone involved.

Characteristics of a Toxic relationship

1. **Manipulation:** One partner exerts control or influence over the other in deceptive or exploitive ways.

2. **Lack of Support:** Partners are unsupportive of each other, often dismissive or derogatory about the other's accomplishments or emotions.

3. **Constant Criticism:** Regular and unwarranted criticism that lowers the partner's self-esteem and fosters insecurity.

4. **Disrespect:** Persistent disrespect towards one's boundaries, feelings, body, or thoughts.

5. **Controlling Behaviors:** Attempts to control the other partner's actions, choices, and interactions with others.

6. **Neglect:** Failing to fulfill the emotional or physical needs of the partner, often leading to feelings of neglect.

7. **Hostility:** Frequent anger, hostility, or resentment creates a pervasive tension and conflict atmosphere.

8. **Dishonesty:** Lack of honesty that erodes trust; this could include lying, hiding things, or deceit.

9. **Isolation:** Efforts to isolate the partner from friends, family, or other supportive networks.

A relationship must not display all these characteristics to be considered toxic. The persistent presence of even a few can harm emotional health and well-being.

CHAPTER 2

They Bring Out Your Toxicity

Destructive relationship patterns can bring out the worst in us, especially when times get tough. It's not unusual to see people showing their negative side or acting in toxic ways when the relationship hits rough patches. Here, we'll talk about how to recognize these behaviors in ourselves, understand where they come from, and learn better ways to manage them. Rather than letting these behaviors run wild and damage our relationships, we can learn to keep them in check and make healthier choices.

When a relationship starts to trigger our toxic traits, it usually follows specific patterns that can turn simple disagreements into serious conflicts. Let's look at two common patterns:

Constant Conflict: Imagine a couple that argue every day about small things like what's for dinner or who forgot to take out the trash. These frequent clashes can add stress and build up resentment. After a while, both partners might start reacting more aggressively or defensively out of habit, even when the issue is trivial.

Jealousy and Control: Picture a partner who gets uneasy whenever their significant other talks to friends or coworkers of the opposite sex. This insecurity might lead them to ask to check their partner's phone messages or social media, crossing personal boundaries and planting seeds of distrust. While this controlling behavior comes from a place of jealousy, it often leads to bigger issues, like constant arguments and emotional distance.

Bringing Up Past Mistakes: Imagine a partner who just can't let go of a past slip-up, like a forgotten anniversary. Each time there's an argument, they bring it up as proof that the other isn't committed or doesn't care enough. This constant reminder can make the other person feel judged and undervalued, often causing them to lash back or shut down defensively.

Ignoring Your Partner's Needs: Think of a situation where one person always puts their own wants first choosing the TV shows every night without a second thought or making social plans without asking for their partner's input. Over time, this can make the other person feel like they don't matter, like their opinions aren't worth considering. This feeling of being invisible can lead to outbursts of frustration or even emotional withdrawal.

Blame Games: Picture a relationship where one partner blames the other for any problem or stress in life. If they had a rough day at work, instead of processing it, they might take it out on their partner, saying they weren't supportive enough. This constant blame can corner the other person, making them defensive or even causing them to fire back, keeping both partners stuck in a cycle of blame and resentment.

Recognizing these patterns is the first step to breaking free of them and building a healthier relationship.

Danger Of Being With The Wrong One

When it comes to choosing a partner, spotting **"Danger of being with the wrong one"** in relationships is essential for any woman. These warning signs are clues that there might be issues that could affect your emotional well-being and the relationship's health. Red flags highlight when something's off and stress the need for a connection built on respect, trust, and understanding.

Communication is key to a strong relationship, so pay attention if your partner consistently avoids tough conversations, dismisses your feelings, or resists open and honest dialogue. This is a big red flag because communication helps both partners feel valued and heard. Without it, the foundation of the relationship weakens, making it hard to build something lasting.

Another major red flag is control. It might start with your partner deciding where you should go, who you should spend time with, or how you spend your day. Control can chip away at your sense of self and independence. Recognizing this behavior early on can help stop a destructive pattern before it takes hold.

Disrespect is also a serious sign to watch for. This can show up as belittling comments, mocking, or intimidation. Respect is the bedrock of any healthy relationship, and without it, the relationship can't truly flourish. Addressing disrespectful behavior quickly is essential to protect your dignity and emotional well-being.

Finally, trust is the true foundation of any healthy relationship. If your partner's behavior is unpredictable or if they seem unclear in their commitment, it can erode trust and create emotional strain. If they're often secretive, lie frequently, or act in ways that make you feel suspicious, these are major red flags signaling a lack of trustworthiness.

Being able to spot and address these signs can help you build a relationship that values you as you are and supports your emotional health.

We all have a past, but unresolved baggage from previous experiences can block the growth of a healthy relationship. When old issues spill into the present, it makes building a solid connection harder. Similarly, a partner who regularly overindulges in substances to the point where it affects daily life or the dynamics of your relationship is a serious red flag. This behavior can lead to bigger issues, including financial strain, legal troubles, and even emotional or physical harm.

Another major concern is when a partner shows little interest in your life, emotions, or needs.

Relationships thrive on mutual care and involvement; when that's missing, it's a clear signal that something's off. Additionally, manipulative behavior, like guilt-tripping or gaslighting, is a serious warning sign. Such tactics can harm your mental health and destabilize the relationship, making it essential to address these behaviors to protect yourself and the integrity of the partnership.

Learning to recognize these red flags helps you engage in relationships that are truly supportive, fulfilling, and respectful. Identifying these signs early on lets you either address the issues constructively or make the difficult decision to walk away. The journey of love is about finding the right match—and understanding when someone isn't. By protecting your emotional well-being, you open yourself to nurturing connections that add real value to your life. Love should uplift and inspire you, and with the right awareness, you can ensure it does.

Staying in a relationship with the wrong person can deeply disrupt personal growth and happiness in many ways. In an incompatible partnership, you may feel constantly drained, with stress, anxiety, and sadness becoming part of daily life. Instead of focusing on personal goals, you might find yourself constantly trying to soothe an unhappy partner or repair emotional rifts. This cycle can pull you away from your own ambitions, hindering your journey toward self-fulfillment and growth.

Being with the wrong partner can also damage your self-image. When you're constantly criticized or belittled, it can slowly chip away at how you see yourself, planting seeds of doubt about your abilities and worth. This relentless negativity can pull you away from your true self, making you question your decisions and undermining your natural confidence.

Differences in life goals can also drive a wedge between partners. For example, if you're focused on building your career while your partner prioritizes a quieter domestic life, these contrasting goals can lead to compromises that make one or both partners feel unfulfilled. Over time, you might find yourself sidelining your dreams, creating a sense of drifting off-course.

The cost of staying in such relationships is high. The time and energy you pour into patching up a misaligned relationship could be used to advance your own growth, explore career paths, or pursue activities that genuinely bring you joy. Recognizing these dynamics allows you to make thoughtful choices about your relationships and life direction.

Having a controlling partner can also restrict your social circle. They might explicitly limit who you can spend time with or demand so much of your energy that you have little left for others. This isolation can cut you off from new ideas and experiences, keeping you from growing and evolving.

Being aware of these patterns helps you make decisions that support your well-being and personal growth. Relationships should elevate you, not hold you back from reaching your potential.

In a relationship like this, it's easy to end up ignoring your own needs. You might stop prioritizing your health, give up hobbies you enjoy, or skip out on activities that make you feel good. Over time, this neglect can take a toll on your physical and mental well-being, causing you to lose sight of who you truly are.

You might also start hiding your real feelings or desires just to keep the peace or make an unsupportive partner happy. This means putting on a mask, keeping you from fully enjoying life and finding true happiness and fulfillment.

Addressing these issues often means taking a close look at your life and finding the courage to make changes that steer you back to being yourself and feeling happy. Recognizing these problems helps you decide whether to keep working on the relationship or consider moving toward a more supportive and fulfilling partnership.

Being with the wrong partner can bring out toxic behaviors, sometimes subtly, sometimes more obviously. A common reaction is becoming defensive to protect yourself. If you're often criticized, misunderstood, or emotionally neglected, you might start using sarcasm, acting passive-aggressively, or even showing open hostility. Over time, these defense mechanisms can become habits, impacting not only this relationship but also other social interactions.

In many cases, stress and resentment are what drive toxic behaviors. When a relationship is full of arguments and negative energy keeps building up, people tend to either lash out, pull away emotionally, or act out of spite. At the time, these reactions might feel like ways to deal with anger and disappointment, but in truth, they just keep the unhealthy cycle going.

Another trap is when you start picking up your partner's bad habits, especially if they're using manipulation, dishonesty, or emotional abuse. Trying to cope with their behavior, you might begin copying these toxic tactics yourself. This can mess with your sense of right and wrong and even affect how you relate to other people in your life.

When you're constantly sacrificing your values or boundaries to keep your partner happy, it can backfire. Putting your needs or morals aside all the time creates inner conflict, which eventually turns to bitterness or worse. It leads to struggles with self-worth and can leave you feeling like you've lost your identity.

In relationships where your emotional needs are brushed aside, you may find yourself looking for validation in ways that aren't healthy. This could mean taking big risks, becoming overly dependent on others, or even manipulating people just to feel valued. These behaviors show that, deep down, you're searching for emotional connection and recognition that you're not getting.

Spotting these issues early can guide you back to a healthier place, where you're more in touch with what you need and believe in. With this awareness, you can seek or build relationships that strengthen your well-being, rather than drain it.

Poor communication adds fuel to the fire in a toxic relationship. When conflicts keep piling up because partners only yell, cut each other off, or flat-out refuse to listen, it only builds frustration and confusion. Without effective communication, misunderstandings grow, and this lack of real connection can lead to behaviors that spill over and impact other parts of your life.

Being isolated from family and friends, whether your partner is pushing for it or it's just a result of the relationship's dynamics, can make you feel even more trapped and dependent. This isolation can drive you to desperate actions as you try to get back a sense of control and connection.

The wrong partner has a strong influence on your life and shows why it's so important to keep relationships healthy. Fixing these issues might mean seeking professional advice, taking time for serious self-reflection, and sometimes asking yourself if the relationship is worth it in the long run. Your well-being—and your peace of mind—depends on it.

Oddly enough, being with the wrong partner can leave you feeling lonely even though you're technically "together." This emotional loneliness kicks in when there's no depth, understanding, or real intimacy in the connection, leaving you feeling unsupported and alone.

When communication between partners stays on the surface or doesn't allow for honesty, sharing your true thoughts and feelings becomes hard. This lack of real conversation can make you feel invisible, as though you're in the relationship physically, but emotionally, you're alone. Without a safe space to express your vulnerabilities, you might feel like you have to keep parts of yourself hidden, deepening the isolation.

If your partner doesn't respect your interests or goals, that, too, can leave you feeling cut off. When they constantly brush off what you're passionate about, it can make you withdraw. This kind of disconnect drains you and holds back your growth because there's no joy from shared experiences or encouragement.

Lastly, loneliness can come from an unbalanced relationship, where one partner calls all the shots, or one person is far more invested than the other. This imbalance can make the less dominant partner feel more like an afterthought than an equal, heightening the feeling of loneliness and detachment.

Sometimes, being with the wrong partner means you end up cut off from friends and family, intentionally or not. This kind of isolation can be a way for them to control you, making you rely on them alone for social interaction and support. And if the relationship itself isn't fulfilling, this dependence feels even more painful.

The deep loneliness that comes from a wrong relationship makes it clear how much it harms your emotional well-being. Recognizing this loneliness is the first step toward addressing the root issues in the relationship—or, if needed, making bigger changes to reclaim a sense of connection and purpose.

Breaking free from the pattern of staying in a bad relationship just to avoid facing the truth takes self-awareness, courage, and a strategic approach. Often, staying comes from a fear of being alone, failing, or having to face the real dynamics at play.

The journey to making healthier choices starts with getting honest with yourself. Knowing your needs, desires, and usual relationship patterns makes it easier to see why you might stick with choices that keep things unfulfilling. This process usually involves self-reflection, journaling, or even having real conversations with trusted friends. Taking time to think through these patterns helps you spot and tackle repeating mistakes.

Building a strong sense of self-worth is key. When you recognize your value, it's less likely you'll settle for a relationship where you're forced into bad decisions. Boosting self-esteem might mean talking to a counselor or joining support groups. These steps help you reach a place where being on your own feels better than staying in a dysfunctional relationship, giving you the strength to choose what's best for your well-being.

Setting clear boundaries is also critical to maintaining your own well-being and creating a healthy dynamic. Boundaries help you show your partner what behaviors you can't accept. If those boundaries are crossed, it's important to address it directly instead of letting things slide or making compromises that cost you in the long run.

Getting clarity often means stepping outside the echo chamber of your relationship. Sometimes, you need insights from people who truly care about you to see things from a fresh angle. This outside perspective can help you look at the relationship more objectively and make decisions that genuinely benefit you, not just ones that feel convenient or temporarily comforting.

Open, assertive communication is essential to prevent misunderstandings and avoid making poor choices just to dodge conflict. When you express your thoughts, feelings, and concerns clearly and respectfully, it helps both of you understand each other better. This open dialogue can lead to choices that benefit you both.

Thinking about the future instead of focusing only on the here and now can also lead to better decisions.

By imagining where you want to be, you can see whether your current relationship supports or holds back your long-term goals.

Using these approaches, you'll find yourself making decisions that genuinely improve your well-being, not out of fear or a sense of obligation. This shift leads to healthier relationships and greater personal fulfillment, setting your life on a path toward more rewarding experiences.

10 Psychological Red Flags To Be Aware Of

In relationships, "red flags" refer to behaviors or signs that indicate potential problems or underlying issues that could compromise the relationship's health and stability. These warning signs suggest that a relationship may not be healthy or may become problematic. Recognizing red flags early can help individuals address concerns or decide how to proceed in a relationship. Here are some common psychological red flags to be aware of:

1. **Excessive Jealousy or Possessiveness:** Intense jealousy or possessive behaviors can indicate insecurity and lead to controlling actions.

2. **Lack of Communication:** Difficulty or unwillingness to communicate about feelings, thoughts, or needs can prevent the development of a deep and trusting relationship.

3. **Disrespectful Behavior:** This can include belittling, mocking, or consistently interrupting the other person, showing a lack of respect for them as an equal partner.

4. **Avoidance of Conflict Resolution:** Avoiding or refusing to address conflicts can accumulate unresolved issues, deteriorating relationship health.

5. **Gaslighting:** A form of manipulation where one partner causes the other to doubt their own perceptions, memories, or sanity.

6. **Substance Abuse:** Excessive use of substances that affect relationship or individual behaviors negatively.

7. **Unreliability:** Consistently failing to meet commitments or being generally unreliable can erode trust and security within the relationship.

8. **Lack of Boundaries:** This includes not respecting personal space, privacy, or the need for independence within the relationship.

9. **History of Unhealthy Relationships:** A pattern of unstable or unhealthy relationships in one's past can indicate unresolved issues that might affect current relationships.

10. **Quick Involvement:** Rushing into emotional intimacy or commitment can sometimes indicate underlying emotional needs that are not addressed healthily.

These red flags are often more apparent as a relationship develops and may require careful consideration and open communication to address effectively. Recognizing and addressing these signs can prevent further emotional distress and promote healthier relationships.

CHAPTER 3

Loneliness Will Do It

Sometimes, the fear of being alone can make people rush into relationships that aren't right for them. But spending time on your own isn't necessarily a bad thing. In fact, it can help you grow stronger and become more independent.

When loneliness kicks in, there's often a pull to fill that empty feeling with any company, even if it's not the best. This can make someone jump into a relationship too quickly, without really checking if the other person is a good fit. The fear of being alone can feel more frightening than sticking around in a relationship that isn't good.

But being alone can actually be a powerful time for personal growth. It's a chance to learn more about yourself, what you enjoy, and what you really want out of life. This can make you stronger and boost your confidence. When you're comfortable on your own, you're more likely to choose a partner because you truly want to be with them—not just to fill a gap.

An abusive partner, on the other hand, can create deep loneliness even within the relationship by isolating you from friends, family, and other support networks. This isolation is often a control tactic. They might limit who you can talk to or spend time with, sometimes making negative comments about your friends or family to build doubt and mistrust. Over time, this cuts off social connections, making you rely more on the abuser and feel even more alone.

Another way an abusive partner creates loneliness is by pulling back emotionally. They may ignore the other person's needs, refuse to listen, or withhold affection as a way to punish. Even if they're there physically, the victim often feels unsupported and alone because their emotional needs are left unmet. This creates an isolated feeling, even when they're not by themselves.

Constant criticism and putting down also adds to loneliness. When someone is always belittled, it wears down their self-esteem and makes them feel unworthy of love and respect. They may start believing they don't deserve better treatment or that others wouldn't want to be around them. This negative self-image makes them feel even more isolated since they may no longer feel comfortable reaching out for help.

An abusive partner may also use gaslighting—making the other person question their own thoughts and feelings. By convincing the victim they're "crazy" or just exaggerating, the abuser causes confusion and self-doubt. This tactic makes the victim feel isolated, as they hesitate to reach out, worrying that others won't believe them.

This kind of loneliness goes beyond just being physically alone; it's a deep sense of emotional disconnection and lack of support. Breaking free from this isolation means recognizing abuse, seeking support from people you trust, and rebuilding your self-worth.

The Loneliness Single Mothers Face in Dating

The loneliness of single mothers face in dating hits different when you see it through their eyes. It's not just about trying to find love; it's about juggling responsibilities that never stop. These women are carrying the weight of being both mom and dad, provider and protector, and still trying to carve out space for their own needs. The reality is a lot of brothers don't step up to the challenge because they see kids and think "too much baggage." That leaves these women out here feeling like their options are slim, like they've got to settle or be alone. And that kind of isolation, man, it's real.

On a deeper level, it's the emotional loneliness that really cuts. Single mothers have been through relationships that didn't work, dreams that got put on hold—and now they're trying to figure out if anyone's going to accept them as they are. There's that constant worry: "If I open up, will this man see my value or just see my situation?" And let's not even talk about the protective instincts they have for their kids. They can't just bring anyone around their babies, so now they're carrying the weight of protecting their heart and their family at the same time. That kind of pressure? It's enough to make anyone shut down.

Then there's the judgment they face from society. The world likes to act like a mother is supposed to give up her happiness for her kids, like she's not supposed to want or need love. When they do step out and date, people start talking, throwing shade, asking, "Shouldn't you be home with your kids?" That kind of scrutiny makes it even harder. So, instead of being celebrated for trying to build something real for themselves, they end up feeling invisible or shamed for wanting what everybody else wants: companionship and love.

For single mothers, the loneliness isn't just about not having a partner—it's about feeling like nobody really gets what they're going through. It's heavy, man. They're out here trying to hold it all together, hoping somebody will see them for the strong, deserving women they are. And when that happens? When they find that person who's ready to show up and stay solid? That's when they can finally breathe and know they're not in this alone anymore.

In relationships, especially when you're a single parent, how a potential partner interacts with your children says a lot about their character and whether they're a good fit for you. A considerate partner will naturally be thoughtful about your responsibilities. They'll ask simple but telling questions, like if you're comfortable arranging a babysitter when you go out or if you'd like to take food home for the kids. These small gestures show they respect the role you play as a parent.

It's also crucial to take time before introducing your children to someone new. Early introductions can confuse or even unsettle kids, especially if the relationship doesn't go the distance. As you spend time dating and getting to know this person, think about how they might fit into your family life. Do they show signs of having a positive influence on your children? Are they secure enough to handle the realities of a blended family, including relationships with your children's other parent?

It's also important to discuss parenting styles and values. If they have children, pay attention to how they treat themselves, as it can reveal a lot about how they'll treat you and yours. Are your approaches to parenting compatible? Do they prioritize the well-being and upbringing of children like you do?

Choosing a partner when you have children means paying attention to how they relate not only to you but also to the most important people in your life—your children. If they don't have children of their own, you need to think carefully. Do you want a man in your life who has never parented? Some women say they want a man with no children, but if you have kids, it's important to make sure he's ready to be in a family setting. You need to ask yourself: does he have the qualities of a good father or stepfather?

If he does have children, watch how he treats them, because it's unlikely he'll treat your children any better. Is he the type to favor his own kids over yours? That's a sign he may not be the right one for your family. Sometimes, you might find yourself liking a man more than his ability to be a father figure for your kids. In that case, the key question to ask yourself is: What will I do if I care for him more than he cares for my children?

When bringing a new partner into your family, especially with the kids involved, the focus should be on how well he connects with and respects your children. This speaks to his capacity to be a supportive partner. Some people just don't have the emotional or practical capacity to handle the realities of a blended family.

Just as you can't fit eight ounces of water into a six-ounce bottle, you can't expect someone without the right capacity to fit into your family dynamic. The right partner for a single parent has to be able to love and care for you and support your role as a parent. They should have the patience, understanding, and affection to embrace your children as part of the family.

The wrong partner might show signs of struggling to connect with or include your children in the bigger picture of your relationship. This is an important sign to watch out for. As the saying goes, "More is caught than taught." Pay close attention to what a potential partner says about your family situation and, more importantly, how they act. When you eventually introduce them to your children, observe how they engage. Actions always speak louder than words, and a real interest in your kids is non-negotiable.

Even if you haven't introduced your children to them yet, your partner should still show genuine interest in hearing about your kids and, at some point, express a desire to meet them. If you've been dating for a year, and they still haven't shown any curiosity about your children or tried to understand that part of your life, it could be a major red flag that they aren't suited for a family role.

Choosing a partner when you have children isn't just about finding someone right for you, but also someone who fits well with your family. The right partner will understand and respect how important your children are in your life and have the ability to fully embrace and support that side of you.

Challenges a single mother faces when dating

Dating as a single mother comes with its own set of problems, rooted in the realities of balancing family, career, and self-care while navigating the unique dynamics of our communities. Here's a look at some of the key struggles many single mothers face

1. **Time Is Not on your Side**

Between working, running the household, and raising kids, time is precious. Carving out space for dating feels almost impossible when you do it alone.

Finding a babysitter, you trust and making sure your kids are good just to grab a coffee and a sandwich with someone can feel like vacation planning.

2. The Babies Come First

Family is everything; for a single mother, her children are her world. Any potential date (man) has to understand that her babies come first—period.

There's always that fear of how someone new might fit into the family or how they might affect your kids.

3. Judgment from the Community

The whispers, the side-eyes, and even the direct questions: "Why are you still single?" or "Don't you think you should focus on your kids instead of dating?" can weigh heavy.

For single Black mothers, there's often a stigma that unfairly paints them as "less-than" even though they're out here holding it all together.

4. Finding Someone Who Gets It

Not everyone is ready to date a woman with kids, especially when those kids are involved in everything from school plays to Saturday morning basketball games.

The pool of men who are open to it and willing to embrace and uplift her family feels small at times.

5. Emotional Baggage

Many single mothers have been through some things—heartbreak, betrayal, or even just the loneliness that comes with raising kids alone.

Trust doesn't come easy, and it can be hard to open up when you've been let down before.

6. When to Introduce the Kids

You can't bring just anyone around your kids. The stakes are too high. The question of "Is this relationship serious enough to introduce them?" weighs heavy.

Protecting your children's emotional well-being is always on your mind, so you move cautiously.

7. Money Talks

Babysitters cost money. Date night costs money. And let's be honest—sometimes you're more focused on paying for school clothes than going out to eat.

There's also that unspoken pressure to be with someone financially stable because, as a single mom, you're already pulling double duty on the finances.

8. No Village to Lean On

The whole "it takes a village" thing? Sometimes the village just isn't there. Without reliable family or friends to help, the logistics of dating can feel impossible.

For many Black moms, the support network they need just doesn't exist—or they hesitate to ask for help.

9. Co-Parenting Drama

If there's a co-parent in the picture, that relationship can add another layer of complexity. Whether it's tension, unresolved feelings, or custody arrangements, it's all part of the equation.

A new partner also has to understand and respect that dynamic, which isn't always easy.

10. Breaking Generational Cycles

A lot of single Black moms are determined not to repeat the patterns they saw growing up. They're looking for healthy love, not just anyone to fill the void.

This determination means being extra cautious and intentional about who they let into their lives—and their kids' lives.

11. Finding Confidence

Sometimes, after years of putting yourself on the back burner, it's hard to remember who you are outside of being "Mom."

Reclaiming your identity and reminding yourself that you deserve love too is a process that takes time and self-reflection.

12. Pressure from All Sides

Family, church folks, even strangers at the beauty supply store always have something to say: "When are you going to settle down?" or "You need a man to help raise those kids."

Unsolicited advice and opinions can make dating feel like an uphill battle.

Despite the struggles, Black single mothers bring strength, wisdom, and unmatched resilience to relationships. They know what they want and what they won't tolerate. When the right one comes along—

someone who understands, uplifts, and supports, they make the most loving and committed partners.

CHAPTER 4

Stop Making Wrong Right

Stop Making Wrong Right is a principle that challenges us to stop justifying actions, choices, or people that don't align with our values, goals, or well-being. Often, we know when something isn't right for us, but fear, loneliness, or the desire for companionship can lead us to ignore red flags and make excuses for what we know is wrong. This mindset can trap us in situations where we sacrifice our peace, self-respect, and even our family's stability just to keep things together. But making wrong right never leads to real happiness or growth.

In relationships, this means being honest about the signs and truths we see in others. For example, if someone doesn't respect your values, your children, or your goals, ignoring these issues won't make them disappear. It's tempting to believe that time will change them or that we can work around their flaws, but doing so only keeps us stuck in a cycle of compromise that often costs us more than we realize. Excuse or justifying poor treatment, lack of respect, or lack of real support from a partner will only create deeper issues and resentment over time.

"Stop making wrong right" also means respecting yourself enough to recognize that you deserve better. It means trusting that, even if it's hard to face the truth or the idea of being alone, you are better off alone than with someone who doesn't add real value to your life. If you're afraid of being alone, remember that being in the wrong relationship can be just as lonely, if not more so. Loneliness doesn't come from being by yourself, it comes from not feeling truly seen, respected, or valued.

For single parents, this principle is even more crucial. Your children watch and learn from your actions, picking up on how you set boundaries and what you're willing to accept. Making wrong right in relationships teaches children that compromise means sacrificing one's dignity or happiness. Instead, by standing firm in your values, you show them the importance of choosing people who honor and support who you are as a person and as a parent.

At its core, stopping the habit of making wrong right is about breaking free from settling for less than what's healthy or good for you. It's a call to be courageous enough to walk away from anything that doesn't serve your well-being and to stop making excuses for behaviors that hurt you or your loved ones. Instead, focus on building a life with people who respect you, align with your values, and are willing to put in the effort to grow with you. It's about choosing peace over pressure, and real companionship over the illusion of connection.

So, stop making wrong right, and start setting a standard for the kind of life and relationships you truly deserve.

What If I'm The Wrong One

Here's a culturally sensitive and straightforward take on the subject, focusing on self-reflection and the importance of mental well-being in relationships:

Before you decide that the man in your life is "The Wrong One," consider the possibility that you might be dealing with some personal challenges that are affecting the relationship. Sometimes, without realizing it, we can bring our own unresolved issues into our relationships. Through psychology, we know that some people aren't in the healthiest mental space to engage in a balanced relationship. Acknowledging this is not about blame but about understanding ourselves better to avoid risking a good relationship by thinking you're with the wrong man when it might be more complex than that.

Personality disorders are complicated and can impact anyone. Certain disorders, though, are often diagnosed more in women. If you recognize any of these traits in yourself, it might be wise to seek therapy to gain a clearer perspective before reentering the dating scene. It's about giving yourself and your future relationships the best chance of success.

The first and perhaps most common is Borderline Personality Disorder (BPD). This condition is marked by intense, unstable emotions, impulsive behaviors, a deep fear of abandonment, and often, rocky relationships. Studies suggest that BPD is diagnosed more often in women, with about 75% of cases being female. Here are a few questions to consider if BPD might be affecting you:

- Do you have a strong fear of being abandoned?
- When angry, do you react yelling or throwing things?
- Have you ever engaged in physical altercations during heated moments?
- Do you often regret things you said or did in the heat of the moment?
- Do you sometimes break off relationships prematurely, only regret it later?
- Do you find yourself dating multiple people as a backup plan in case one relationship ends?

If any of these questions resonate with you, there may be a chance you're experiencing some symptoms related to BPD. Seeking therapy isn't about labeling yourself, it's about gaining tools and insights to handle your emotions in a way that strengthens your relationships and brings you peace.

Understanding and addressing these challenges allows you to approach future relationships with a clear and healthy mindset. Remember, working through personal challenges isn't a weakness; it's a step toward building the life and relationships you deserve.

Women who struggle with Histrionic Personality Disorder (HPD) tend to show a pattern of excessive emotionality and attention-seeking behavior. This condition can lead a person to feel uneasy or even distressed when they're not the center of attention. Research indicates that HPD may be diagnosed more often in women than in men. Recognizing some of the traits linked to HPD can be a step toward greater self-awareness, which helps in building balanced and healthy relationships.

If you're wondering whether this could apply to you, think about how you behave in social situations. For instance, do you find yourself wearing attention-grabbing outfits that might be seen as provocative, then feel surprised or offended if others respond to you in a suggestive way? In your mind, you may be seeking attention, but not necessarily advances. This is one-way HPD can manifest—the desire to be noticed without wanting things to go further.

Another example is feeling uneasy in social gatherings if the attention isn't on you. You might find yourself getting upset when no one is talking to you or when you're not speaking. Feeling uncomfortable when you're not the center of the conversation or needing to be heard at all times are common signs.

HPD isn't about blaming anyone but about recognizing patterns that may affect your well-being and relationships. Seeking support from a therapist can help you understand these behaviors, find healthy ways to connect with others, and create stronger, more fulfilling relationships. Addressing such issues can be empowering, leading to personal growth and a sense of inner peace.

Women with Dependent Personality Disorder (DPD) often have a strong need to rely on others and can feel uncomfortable when doing things alone. This can manifest as constantly seeking validation, and without it, they may feel lost or unsure of themselves. Traditionally, DPD has been diagnosed more frequently in women, though some experts argue that cultural expectations and societal norms have played a role in pushing women toward this kind of dependency.

On the other hand, Avoidant Personality Disorder (APD) can make individuals feel inadequate and highly sensitive to criticism, especially from loved ones. Women with APD often avoid situations where they fear judgment or disapproval. They may find it hard to handle criticism from those they care about and might seek reassurance to feel secure. While APD affects both men and women, some studies suggest it's slightly more reported in women, possibly due to how differently symptoms are perceived in each gender.

It's worth noting that the diagnosis of personality disorders can sometimes be shaped by cultural and gender norms, influencing how symptoms are understood and reported for men versus women. This cultural lens can impact both diagnosis and personal reflection. Before labeling a partner as "The Wrong One," it's crucial for every woman to look inward and consider her own contributions to the relationship. Taking accountability and seeking help if needed are important steps before continuing to pursue new relationships. This reflection can empower women to enter relationships from a place of self-awareness and strength, ultimately leading to healthier connections.

The Psychological Impact of Breakups in Relationships

Breakups in relationships can have profound psychological effects on the individuals involved. Psychologically, the end of a relationship can set off a range of emotional responses, often mirroring the stages of grief we go through when dealing with loss. This comparison isn't surprising, as breakups involve the loss of a significant bond and shared experiences, which can leave a deep void.

Just as in grief, the end of a relationship can lead to feelings of denial, anger, bargaining, depression, and, eventually, acceptance. Denial may come first, where one or both partners struggle to accept that the relationship is truly over. This can lead to a sense of disbelief, as the mind attempts to process the new reality. Anger can then follow, as unresolved emotions and disappointments surface, often directed at either oneself or the other person.

Bargaining is another common reaction, where individuals may replay situations in their minds, wishing they had acted differently or hoping for a way to "fix" things. This stage can be particularly challenging, as it involves the hope that things might go back to how they were. Depression often comes after bargaining, with feelings of sadness and emptiness as one faces the finality of the breakup. It's normal to feel moments of isolation or loneliness during this stage, as the absence of the partner is more deeply felt.

Finally, with time, many people reach acceptance. In this stage, they start to make peace with the breakup, realizing that the relationship ended for a reason. Acceptance allows for a healthier outlook on the future and opens up space for personal growth.

Understanding these impacts can help in navigating the complex emotions that come with breakups. Knowing that these responses are part of a natural grieving process allows individuals to take the time they need to heal, seek support, and eventually move forward with greater self-awareness and resilience. This process can also be an opportunity for reflection, helping individuals gain insights that prepare them for healthier relationships in the future.

Emotional Turbulence and Grief:
The immediate aftermath of a breakup is often marked by an emotional upheaval that feels both intense and overwhelming. This period brings a wave of strong emotions—sadness, anger, confusion, and

loneliness—each reflecting a unique part of the grieving process when a significant relationship comes to an end.

Sadness is one of the most immediate and common feelings. This emotion often stems from the loss of companionship and the deep emotional bond shared with a partner. When a relationship ends, it can feel as if a loved one has passed away. Everything that was shared—affection, love, day-to-day conversations, and inside jokes—suddenly disappeared. Added to this is the grief over a shared future that now no longer exists; the plans, dreams, and moments that were envisioned are no longer possible, intensifying sadness.

Anger can arise from a variety of sources. Sometimes, it's directed at the partner, particularly if there was betrayal, dishonesty, or any sense of unfairness in the breakup. In other cases, anger may be self-directed, stemming from frustration over perceived wasted time and energy. Unresolved conflicts and lingering issues from the relationship can also feed this anger. Psychologically, anger can serve as a defense mechanism, a way to feel empowered and protect against the vulnerability of hurt. However, if not managed well, anger can delay the healing process, keeping one trapped in pain rather than moving forward.

Confusion is also a natural response, as individuals try to make sense of what went wrong. This period may involve replacing conversations, interactions, and decisions in search of clarity. It's common to wonder about the signs missing or to question what could have been done differently. These "what ifs" and "whys" can turn into endless cycles of rumination, complicating the journey to closure and making it difficult to move past the relationship.

Loneliness is often the most challenging part of a breakup. The absence of a partner leaves a tangible void in daily life, especially when a person has grown used to sharing the details of their day, big and small. The companionship that once filled their life is suddenly gone, leaving a gap in routines, social activities, and emotional support. This loneliness can feel profound, as the comfort of partnership is replaced with an unfamiliar solitude.

Each of these emotions—sadness, anger, confusion, and loneliness—is a natural response to the loss of a meaningful connection. Recognizing these feelings as part of a grieving process can help individuals understand that healing takes time. This awareness also opens the door for personal growth, allowing one to explore new routines, discover self-worth, and prepare for healthier relationships in the future.

Relationship loneliness often arises from a significant emotional, physical, or mental disconnect between partners. This type of loneliness doesn't happen overnight but usually develops slowly due to underlying issues that may go unnoticed until the distance feels overwhelming. One of the most common causes is a lack of emotional intimacy. Emotional intimacy is about feeling safe to share thoughts, feelings, and vulnerabilities with your partner. When this sense of safety fades, partners may feel isolated, as though they can't open up or that their emotional expressions are being ignored. Even if they're together physically, the absence of an emotional bond can leave them feeling profoundly alone.

Communication breakdowns are another major cause of loneliness. Communication is the backbone of a healthy relationship, as it allows partners to share love, express needs, and discuss concerns. When communication falters due to misunderstandings, unresolved conflicts, or a lack of openness, it can create a significant emotional divide. Without effective communication, partners can struggle to connect in a meaningful way, leading to a sense of isolation even when they're together.

Life changes can also play a big role in relationship loneliness. Major shifts, such as moving to a new city, changing careers, or having children, can reshape the dynamics of a relationship. If these changes lead to feelings of being unsupported or misunderstood, they can increase feelings of isolation. Often, in adapting to new roles or responsibilities, partners might unknowingly neglect their connection, not realizing the impact until the emotional gap becomes substantial.

Recognizing these causes of loneliness within a relationship can be the first step toward reconnecting and rebuilding emotional intimacy. By addressing the lack of communication, making time for shared experiences, and offering support during life changes, partners can work together to bridge the gap and restore a sense of closeness and understanding.

Personal growth or changes within one or both partners can lead to a sense of loneliness in relationships. As people grow and evolve, their needs, interests, and values often shift. When these changes aren't shared openly or happen at different paces, they can create a silent divide. One or both partners may feel as though the other no longer fully understands or connects with them, resulting in a feeling of loneliness even when they're physically together.

Recognizing early signs of loneliness and addressing underlying issues through honest communication and empathy can be essential steps to prevent further disconnection. By making a conscious effort to nurture the relationship, partners can reconnect and bridge the gap. Actively working to maintain the bond that first brought them together—by sharing their evolving goals, values, and experiences—helps reinforce their connection and reduce feelings of isolation.

When relationships end, the resulting emotions can be profound, manifesting as symptoms of depression and anxiety. These intense feelings are natural responses to the loss of an emotional anchor. Depression may show up as persistent sadness, a lack of interest in activities once enjoyed, appetite or sleep disturbances, and a general sense of withdrawal. Anxiety can be presented through increased nervousness, difficulty concentrating, restlessness, and excessive worry about what lies ahead.

The sudden lack of stability, emotional, and sometimes logistical, often leaves individuals feeling unmoored. The relationship that once provided comfort and structure is gone, forcing one to navigate life without that support. This can disrupt one's sense of normalcy and amplify feelings of anxiety and depression.

Adapting to these new realities requires courage and a willingness to confront and manage intense emotions. Rebuilding a sense of independence and identity outside the relationship is a critical step in the healing journey. Although challenging, this process of self-discovery and personal growth offers the chance to create a stable, fulfilling life that isn't reliant on any one relationship, ultimately fostering resilience and a deeper sense of self-worth.

Self-Esteem and Identity Reevaluation:

A breakup can deeply affect one's self-esteem and self-concept, as relationships often shape how we see ourselves. While in a relationship, people commonly define themselves in terms of their roles within the partnership—who they are as a partner, shared goals, and a combined identity. When the relationship ends, individuals may experience a loss of identity, finding themselves in unfamiliar territory as they try to redefine who they are outside of the relationship.

This period of re-evaluation can be challenging and even distressing. The sudden void left by a partner can lead to feelings of emptiness and a diminished sense of self-worth, especially if the relationship was central to one's identity. Self-esteem may take a hit as individuals struggle with doubts and insecurities, questioning their own value and what they bring to a partnership. These feelings can be intensified if the breakup triggers self-blame or if there was a dependency on the partner for validation.

However, this time of change can also open the door to personal growth and self-discovery. Without the influence of the relationship, individuals have an opportunity to explore their true interests, strengths, and values. Rebuilding a sense of self outside the relationship allows for a more authentic and resilient identity to emerge. This process, though difficult, can lead to renewed self-confidence, greater independence, and clarity about what one truly wants in life and future relationships.

The outcome of this journey often depends on the support systems available and individual coping mechanisms. Friends, family, and sometimes professional counseling can play crucial roles in helping individuals process emotions, rebuild confidence, and set personal goals. Coping strategies like self-reflection, setting new goals, and focusing on activities that bring joy and fulfillment can ease the transition.

Ultimately, while a breakup can feel like a loss of self, it also offers a chance to reconnect with one's core identity, separate from any relationship. Embracing this period of change with a mindset geared toward self-growth can transform a painful experience into a foundation for a stronger, more self-assured future.

Behavioral Changes:

Behavioral changes are common after a breakup, as individuals try to process and manage their emotions. These changes can range from shifts in daily routines to more extreme reactions. For some, a breakup disrupts sleeping and eating patterns, leading to insomnia, oversleeping, loss of appetite, or overeating. These physical changes reflect the emotional turmoil within and can leave individuals feeling physically drained and mentally unbalanced.

In some cases, people may turn to risk-taking behaviors to escape or numb the emotional pain. This might include impulsive spending, substance use, or engaging in unsafe activities. While these actions might provide temporary relief, they can have serious consequences and may lead to further feelings of guilt or regret, adding to the emotional burden.

Another common response is social withdrawal. Feeling emotionally raw, many individuals isolate themselves, withdrawing from social activities and avoiding friends and family. While solitude can sometimes provide space to reflect, prolonged isolation can intensify feelings of loneliness and depression. Without the support of loved ones, it's easy to feel stuck in negative thoughts, making it harder to find a path forward.

On the opposite end of the spectrum, some individuals cope by throwing themselves into activities, work, or social events as a way to distract themselves from the pain. This can serve as a temporary escape, but if overdone, it can lead to burnout or avoidance behaviors. Rather than processing emotions, constant activity can delay healing and lead to exhaustion, leaving individuals feeling emotionally drained when the distractions inevitably fade.

Navigating these behavioral changes is about finding a balance. Giving yourself time to grieve, while also staying connected with loved ones, can help manage the intense emotions that follow a breakup. Healthy coping mechanisms—like physical exercise, journaling, or engaging in hobbies—can provide a constructive outlet for processing feelings without leading to burnout or self-destructive behaviors.

Ultimately, being mindful of these behaviors and choosing paths that support healing rather than avoidance can help individuals regain a sense of stability and start building a healthier foundation for personal growth

Long-Term Psychological Effects:

The long-term psychological effects of a breakup can differ greatly from one person to another. For some, the experience, although painful, becomes an opportunity for personal growth and increased resilience. These individuals often take the time to reflect on what went wrong and develop a better understanding of their relationship needs, values, and boundaries. This period of self-reflection can be transformative, leading to stronger self-awareness and clearer intentions for future relationships. With newly acquired coping skills and a strengthened sense of self, they often emerge more resilient and better prepared to navigate future emotional challenges.

However, for others, the aftermath of a breakup can have more lasting and challenging effects, especially if the breakup was particularly traumatic or if it followed a series of similar painful experiences. Individuals with preexisting mental health issues, such as depression or anxiety, may find that the breakup intensifies their struggles, making it harder to move forward. In some cases, the lingering impact can lead to chronic anxiety and depression, where individuals may feel stuck in a loop of self-doubt, sadness, and diminished self-worth.

A history of difficult breakups can also create a kind of relationship phobia, where the fear of emotional pain becomes so intense that individuals avoid future relationships altogether. This fear can limit one's willingness to open up to others, as they become guarded to protect themselves from potentially hurt. Over time, this avoidance may impact on social connections, leading to feelings of isolation and a deepened sense of loneliness.

Recognizing and addressing these potential long-term effects is essential for healing. Therapeutic support, whether through counseling or support groups, can be incredibly helpful in working through complex emotions and rebuilding confidence. With the right tools and support, individuals can learn to process their pain constructively, allowing for healing and future connections that feel both safe and fulfilling.

Ultimately, the way individuals respond to a breakup in the long term depends on various factors, including personal resilience, support systems, and the willingness to seek help if needed. While some may face more difficult emotional obstacles, many find that the journey through heartbreak, though challenging, brings new clarity, strength, and growth.

Recovery and Moving Forward:

Recovery from a breakup involves working through emotional and behavioral stages to rebuild a sense of self and independence. This journey often begins with reestablishing individuality and rediscovering what makes you unique outside the context of a relationship. During this time, focusing on self-care is essential—whether it's taking time to exercise, practicing mindfulness, or engaging in hobbies that bring joy and fulfillment. These activities help to ground you and remind you of the importance of caring for yourself.

Seeking social support from friends and family can also make a big difference. Trusted loved ones can offer comfort, perspective, and a listening ear, which can ease feelings of isolation. For some, talking with a therapist or counselor provides valuable guidance and professional support, helping to process emotions and identify healthy coping mechanisms.

Over time, these steps can empower individuals to move forward with a clearer sense of self. Many find that, with patience and self-reflection, they emerge from a breakup with a deeper understanding of their own needs, values, and goals. This clarity can set the foundation for healthier, more fulfilling future relationships.

Ultimately, understanding the psychological impacts of breakups gives individuals the insight and tools needed to navigate this challenging life event. While the process is rarely easy, it leads to recovery and can be a significant period of personal growth. By embracing this journey, individuals not only heal but often discover new strengths and a renewed sense of purpose, ready to move forward with resilience and hope.

CHAPTER 5

When The Wrong One Comes Vs When The Right One Comes

How to identify the Wrong One

Awoman can tell when the wrong man comes into her life because she's got that intuition, that inner voice that won't let her ignore the signs. She's learned from experience and the wisdom passed down from others to spot the patterns that don't sit right. The wrong man might come in talking a good game, but over time, his actions start showing who he really is. He's inconsistent, doesn't respect her boundaries, and isn't willing to communicate in a way that builds trust. Instead of adding to her peace, he disrupts it, making her question whether he's really about her or just about himself.

The signs get clearer when you look at the bigger picture. She's probably seen or heard enough to know when someone's not serious about stepping up. The wrong man might try to dim her light, downplay her accomplishments, or use slick words to manipulate her emotions. He might present himself as a leader or a protector, but when it's time to follow through, he's nowhere to be found. Whether it's being financially irresponsible, emotionally unavailable, or dismissive of her goals, he shows through his actions that he's not ready for a real partnership.

Another way she spots the wrong man is by how he handles the people and values that matter most to her—her family, her kids (if she has them), or her faith. A man who can't respect those things, or worse, competes with them, shows he's not aligned with her vision of what a relationship should be. For a woman who understands the importance of building a legacy and staying true to her roots, that's a dealbreaker.

When the wrong man steps into her life, her spirit feels off, and her intuition starts sounding the alarm. She knows the difference between what's real and what's just talk. It takes strength to recognize it and even more to walk away, but she does it because she knows her worth. She's holding out for the man who's ready to show up for her, for her family, and for the life she's building. She doesn't settle—she knows the right man will come when the time is right.

When The Right One Comes

When the right one comes into her life, everything feels different—it's a peace she hasn't known in a long time. He doesn't just talk about being there for her; he shows up in real, tangible ways. His actions match his words, and he's consistent in how he treats her, her goals, and the things that matter most to her. She doesn't have to wonder where she stands because he makes it clear through his respect, his support, and his willingness to invest in the relationship. With him, there's no guessing, no confusion—just an undeniable sense of partnership and alignment.

The right man recognizes her worth without needing her to prove it. He's not intimidated by her strength or her independence but instead celebrates it. He steps in to lighten her load, not add to it, and he's intentional about understanding her world. Whether she's a mother, a career woman, or someone pursuing her dreams, he honors her journey and fits into it without trying to overshadow it. He brings stability and security, emotionally, spiritually, and even practically, in ways that make her feel safe to be vulnerable.

He also values the pillars of her life—her family, her children (if she has them), her faith, and her community. He doesn't compete with these things; he embraces them. The right man is willing to integrate himself into her world while still respecting the boundaries and responsibilities she holds close. He makes an effort to understand what drives her, what brings her joy, and what challenges her, and he stands by her as a partner ready to build something solid.

When the right one comes, her spirit feels at ease. There's no anxiety, no second-guessing—just a deep sense of peace that this is the man who sees her fully and loves her completely. Together, they don't just survive; they thrive. She knows she can trust him, lean on him, and grow with him because he's not just about the relationship—he's about building a future with her. The right man doesn't just step into her life; he steps up, proving every day that he's exactly who she's been waiting for.

Signs the Relationship is not working

When a relationship starts to mess with your peace of mind, personal safety, and overall well-being, it crosses the line from being just a "tough patch" to a real-life nightmare. This change doesn't just hit you one day—it builds up slowly, with warning signs along the way that the relationship is becoming harmful.

One of the first signs is the constant arguments that never seem to get anywhere. If you're always fighting, and nothing is really resolved, it creates a stressful atmosphere. The relationship starts to feel like a battlefield, where even the smallest issues can lead to a big blowout. Living in that tension, day in and day out, can be exhausting, making you feel anxious and constantly on edge, with peace and comfort nowhere in sight.

Emotional abuse is a deeper sign that things have taken a dangerous turn. Emotional abuse shows manipulation, constant criticism, threats, or gaslighting—where you start to doubt your own reality. These tactics can break down your confidence and make you feel powerless over time. It's subtle at first, but eventually, you start questioning your own self-worth.

This type of abuse makes it hard to find the strength to leave because it chips away at your confidence bit by bit.

Physical abuse, though, is obviously red flag. When someone lays hands on you, it's a clear sign the relationship is not just unhealthy but dangerous. Physical abuse isn't just a threat to your health; it destroys the trust and safety a relationship should provide. Whether it's emotional or physical, abuse of any kind takes away the security and growth you deserve.

Noticing these signs can be tough, especially when things change gradually. But recognizing them is the first step. Reaching out for support from friends, family, or a professional is key to breaking free from this toxic situation. Leaving this kind of relationship isn't just about getting some peace back, it's about claiming your safety, your self-respect, and a chance at a happier, healthier life.

When one partner tries to control every aspect of your life—who you hang out with, what you spend money on, or even the smallest daily decisions, the relationship starts feeling more like a prison than a partnership. This kind of control often leads to isolation. Slowly, you're cut off from friends and family, leaving you to rely on just that one person, which makes you even more vulnerable.

Neglect is another factor that turns a relationship into a nightmare. When your basic needs—emotional, physical, or even just simple respect—are ignored or brushed aside, it creates deep unhappiness. You might feel like you're invisible, with no one listening or caring about what you're going through. This neglect shows up in the lack of real communication, no affection, or little support, leaving you feeling lonely and unimportant.

One of the most damaging effects of a toxic relationship is the loss of who you are. When your partner constantly overrides your choices or you feel the need to change who you are just to avoid a fight or keep peace, it eats away at your identity. Over time, you start forgetting what you once stood for, what you enjoyed, or even what your dreams were.

The stress of being in a relationship like this can also take a serious toll on your health. Anxiety, depression, sleepless nights, or even physical illnesses can creep in. When your body and mind are suffering because of relationship stress, it's a sure sign that things have gotten serious.

Lastly, when fear becomes your main reaction to your partner—whether it's fear of violence, verbal attacks, or emotional manipulation, the relationship has crossed the line. At that point, it's no longer a place of safety or love, but a source of dread.

When all these issues come together, the relationship ends up becoming a serious obstacle in your life. Spotting these warning signs early on and reaching out for support, whether from friends, family, or professionals—is essential to protect your well-being.

Many people end up in relationships they want but don't necessarily need, often driven by emotions, social expectations, or simply not knowing themselves well enough yet.

At first, the attraction can be strong, sparked by chemistry, a partner's personality, or just the thrill of a new romance. These types of relationships give you that instant high, making you feel desired, which feels good in the short run. You might be drawn to someone who fits the "ideal" image—attractive, charming, successful—without really considering if they can support your deeper emotional and mental needs.

Society and culture also shape our relationship choices more than we might realize. There's often pressured to find a partner who fits a certain social or financial status, even if they might not be a good match for who we truly are. Sometimes, friends and family can unintentionally push us toward relationships that look good on the outside but lack the emotional depth or shared values that matter in the long term.

Not knowing yourself well is another big factor. Without a clear sense of your own needs, values, and goals, it's hard to really understand what you need from a relationship. Often, people get into relationships based on what they think they should want, shaped by social pressures or unresolved issues, like low self-esteem or past hurts. This can lead to picking partners for reasons that only meet immediate needs, like avoiding loneliness or fitting in socially, rather than looking for true, long-term compatibility.

The excitement of being in a relationship you want but don't actually need tends to fade once the reality of misalignment starts to show. Over time, that initial attraction and thrill can give way to the realization that deeper needs—like emotional support, understanding, and shared goals—just aren't being met. This often leads to dissatisfaction and feeling disconnected, which makes you rethink what's truly important in a partner.

Recognizing this misalignment usually takes some self-reflection and honest communication with your partner about needs and expectations. Talking with a therapist or counselor can also be helpful in figuring out and voicing your needs, which makes it easier to make better relationship choices moving forward. This self-awareness, combined with guidance, can pave the way for stronger, more fulfilling relationships that align with who you really are and what you value most.

People often miss the warning signs in relationships because of emotional investment, hope, denial, and sometimes simply not knowing what a healthy relationship should look like. These factors can make it easy to ignore or explain away red flags that might signal deeper issues.

A common reason people overlook these signs is because of their strong attachment to their partner.

When you're deeply in love or emotionally invested, you tend to see everything through "rose-colored glasses." This bias makes it easy to focus on the positives, brush off negative behaviors as one-offs, or excuse them as reactions to temporary stress. This emotional attachment creates a kind of blind spot, where your desire to make things work overshadows your ability to judge whether the relationship is actually healthy.

Denial is another big reason warning signs are missing. Admitting that the relationship might be in trouble is tough, especially when you've put a lot of time, energy, and hope into it. It's often easier to downplay or ignore the problems, convincing yourself that things will get better with time. This avoidance can keep you from dealing with serious issues early on, which can make things worse in the long run.

Some people simply don't know what signs to watch out for in a troubled relationship. Without a clear understanding of what's healthy versus unhealthy, behaviors like extreme jealousy, control, or disrespect can be misunderstood as normal—or even as signs of love. This lack of awareness often comes from past experiences, like growing up in a dysfunctional family or being in previous relationships where unhealthy dynamics were treated as normal.

Hope can also make it easy to miss the signs. Many people hold onto the belief that they can change their partner or that their partner will change because of their love and effort. While that kind of hopefulness is admirable, it can sometimes cloud judgment, leading to staying in a relationship that's actually causing harm.

To spot the warning signs in a relationship, it often helps to step back and look at things objectively. Talking it through with trusted friends, family, or even professionals can offer fresh insight and the support needed to make the best choices.

CHAPTER 6

Fear of Rejection – Emotional Transparency and Vulnerability

When a woman is looking for a meaningful connection with a man, she often values his ability to be vulnerable. Vulnerability from a man means being open about his feelings—sharing his thoughts, fears, and desires openly with his partner. It involves dropping the guard, being real about his struggles, and trusting her with these personal truths. Vulnerability also means he's willing to admit when he doesn't have all the answers, isn't afraid to ask for help, and can take feedback without getting defensive.

This kind of openness helps create a stronger, more trusting relationship, building a foundation of honesty and mutual support that many women genuinely value. But it's important to recognize that being vulnerable doesn't always come easy for men. Society often pressures men to be strong and "unbreakable." Bad experiences in past relationships can also make it hard to open up again. And personal fears about being seen as weak can keep men from sharing their true selves.

Despite these challenges, many women want this level of openness because it improves communication, deepens the emotional bond, and builds a more secure, supportive relationship. When a man is willing to be vulnerable, it shows strength and confidence, both in himself and in the relationship. This openness invites the same level of trust from his partner, creating a deeper connection between them.

Navigating vulnerability can be especially challenging for women who've faced cultural and socio-economic struggles. History and stereotypes have often portrayed women as needing to be strong and always in control. Against a backdrop of marginalization, any show of vulnerability can feel risky—sometimes even threatening their safety, social standing, or personal security.

In many communities, toughness, stoicism, and self-reliance are highly valued traits. They're seen as essential tools for coping with the bigger challenges that women often face. Showing emotions, then, can sometimes feel like a luxury or even a risk, clashing with these deeply held values. Add to that the heavy expectation on women to be caregivers and nurturers and sharing personal fears or emotional needs can sometimes feel like failing in these roles.

In these spaces, unity and collective strength are seen as vital for survival and resilience, so personal vulnerability might seem like a weakness, even if it's not. This perception can make it harder for individuals to talk about their emotional struggles without feeling they're going against the resilience of their community. But despite these pressures, creating safe spaces where women can express their feelings is essential. These environments can help break down limiting stereotypes and foster a healthier, more supportive atmosphere, where openness is viewed as a strength, enriching both personal relationships and the overall well-being of the community.

Mental health issues carry a lot of stigma, often made worse by a deep-rooted distrust in medical systems due to a history of mistreatment. This distrust can stop people from opening up about their struggles or reaching out for mental health support. For many, hiding vulnerability has become a way to protect themselves from discrimination, since showing vulnerability in public can sometimes lead to misunderstandings or even put them at risk.

In relationships, the fear of rejection when opening up about emotional struggles runs deep. This fear isn't just about personal rejection but also about being judged by society and reinforcing negative stereotypes. For groups that have historically been seen in a negative light, there's an extra sensitivity about how they're perceived. Opening up about struggles or weaknesses can feel especially risky, as it might seem to "prove" harmful stereotypes. This fear can make it even harder to show their true selves—including personal flaws or emotional challenges—since doing so could lead not only to rejection from their partners but also to harsh judgment from society.

Expectations from family and community to always be strong and resilient leaders can make the fear of rejection even more intense. In cultures where showing emotions is often seen as a weakness, the stakes for being open and vulnerable are especially high. This pressure makes people hesitant to show any sign of what might be perceived as weakness.

Past experiences of rejection also shape how comfortable someone feels with vulnerability. If someone has opened up before and faced rejection, especially if it seemed to confirm negative stereotypes or fears, they're likely to hesitate before being vulnerable again. This can create a cycle where fear of rejection holds back real emotional expression, making it hard to build deeper, more trusting relationships.

So, the fear of rejection has many layers, mixing personal relationship dynamics with bigger worries about judgment from society and the weight of cultural expectations. Overcoming this fear often requires personal courage, the support of a partner who truly understands, and broader cultural changes that challenge the stereotypes fueling these fears.

For people who have had to fight hard for their sense of agency and respect, control becomes a vital part of who they are and their emotional security. Being vulnerable—letting down defenses and opening up—can feel risky, especially in a society that equates masculinity with strength and control. This pressure is even greater when racial stereotypes paint individuals as either "tough" or "dangerous," making vulnerability seem like giving up the hard-won control they've built in their personal and public lives.

In African American communities, resilience has often been a necessity in the face of systemic challenges. For many women, this has meant building a facade of toughness and maintaining control as a shield against the vulnerabilities that racism and inequality expose. Opening up emotionally can feel like a threat to this resilience, a reminder of past struggles, and a risk of being vulnerable to the same oppressive forces they've spent so long fighting against.

The complex relationship between control and vulnerability is also shaped by personal experiences. For those who have faced trauma or betrayal—especially when these experiences connect to their racial identity—the risk of opening up can feel especially intense. Losing control in these cases isn't just about feeling emotionally exposed; it's wrapped up in a bigger struggle for dignity and self-preservation in a society that can feel hostile.

Working through this fear of losing control goes beyond just personal growth. It involves rethinking how femininity, power, and vulnerability all come together within the experiences of African American women. It means finding spaces and relationships where being open with emotions isn't seen as losing control but as a sign of strength, which can lead to real connection and healing. This process of redefining vulnerability as a form of empowerment is key for personal growth and building supportive, understanding relationships.

For many African American women, expressing emotional vulnerability can be particularly tough because of the cultural and family dynamics they grew up in. In these environments, holding back emotions is often encouraged as a way to handle societal pressures and the challenges within their communities and families. If a woman grows up where showing emotions is discouraged and femininity is tied to toughness, she might find it hard to embrace and express vulnerability later on.

The suppression of emotional expression among African American women has deep historical roots. In the past, showing too much emotion could expose them to serious risks, including physical harm. Because of this, generations of women learned to guard their emotions as a way to protect themselves and their families. This emotional toughness often gets passed down from mothers to daughters, sometimes without even realizing it.

On top of that, many African American women live in social environments marked by systemic bias, racial profiling, and discrimination, where they're expected to maintain a composed exterior. In these situations, showing vulnerability can feel like revealing a weakness that others might exploit. So, their unfamiliarity with opening up emotionally isn't just a personal issue, it's part of a long-standing survival strategy shaped by racial and cultural challenges.

For African American women caught in this cycle of emotional suppression, the challenge isn't just about learning to be vulnerable. It's also about redefining what strength and femininity mean to include the courage to express emotions. Breaking this cycle requires finding or creating supportive spaces where vulnerability is understood, valued, and seen as a sign of strength. This shift is essential for their emotional well-being and the health of their relationships, allowing them to build deeper connections and live a more authentic, fulfilling life.

For African American women, the scars left by past trauma or betrayal can have a big impact on their willingness to be vulnerable in relationships. These experiences, whether from childhood, past relationships, or broader social interactions, often create a strong sense of caution around emotional openness.

Childhood experiences are a big factor in shaping how vulnerability is viewed. In many African American communities, systemic challenges can disrupt family life and community safety, leading to feelings of abandonment, mistrust, and betrayal from a young age. Kids who grow up seeing broken promises, inconsistent care, or the failures of systems meant to protect them often learn to guard their emotions as a way to protect themselves.

This guarded approach often spills over into adulthood, especially in romantic relationships. Society expects us to keep up a tough, unbreakable front, making it even harder to open up. For African American women who've faced betrayal or letdowns after being vulnerable, it can make them feel like showing their true selves only brings pain and rejection. This struggle becomes even tougher with stereotypes that paint vulnerability as a weakness, building yet another wall to break down.

Dealing with these personal and societal blocks to openness is no small feat. It takes healing in places where feelings are understood, and fears aren't brushed aside. Rebuilding trust after being hurt is a slow journey—it's about learning that not everyone will take advantage of your openness and realizing that letting your guard down can actually bring deeper, more meaningful relationships.

For African American women, the hesitation around depending on someone emotionally is often shaped by cultural expectations and real-world pressures. In a world that's often been stacked against them, values like independence and resilience have been vital to survive. In this light, relying on someone else emotionally can feel risky, almost like putting yourself in a vulnerable, even financially risky, position.

This hesitation to lean on others emotionally is also tied to harmful racial stereotypes that either unfairly label African American women as too dependent or not worthy of support. These stereotypes push them to build an image of independence and self-reliance, standing strong to fight back against these negative labels.

In many African American families and communities, resilience and self-reliance are core values—they're about-facing adversity on your own terms. This cultural mindset often treats emotional dependence as letting go of that essential strength. Many African American women find themselves torn between wanting close, supportive relationships and the pressure to live up to community standards of strength and resilience.

The key challenge is to redefine emotional openness, not as a step toward dependency, but as an essential part of healthy interdependence. Emotional connections should be seen as sources of strength, not signs of weakness. Shifting this perspective requires a cultural transformation both within the African American community and in society at large. It calls for a broader understanding of femininity that embraces vulnerability and mutual support. This change is crucial for strengthening personal relationships and breaking down harmful stereotypes and social expectations.

For African American women, the fear of dependency that comes with emotional openness in relationships is deeply rooted in cultural norms and the harsh reality of systemic pressures. In a society marked by discrimination and marginalization, qualities like independence and resilience have been essential defenses. In this environment, emotional dependence can feel like a vulnerability—or even a financial risk.

This hesitation around emotional dependence also traces back to stubborn stereotypes that wrongly paint African American women as either too reliant or undeserving of support. These stereotypes make it clear why so many feel the need to project a strong, independent image to push back against these harmful views.

Plus, in many African American families and communities, there's a heavy emphasis on showing strength and proving you can handle life's struggles solo. This cultural mindset often sees emotional dependence as giving up the power to tackle challenges on your own. This view can create an inner conflict, with many African American women caught between wanting close, supportive relationships and the pressure to live up to community expectations of resilience and femininity.

The real challenge here is shifting how we see emotional openness—not as a weakness or a step toward dependency, but as a key part of balanced, healthy relationships. Emotional connections should be seen as strengths, not soft spots. Getting to this point will take a cultural change, both within the African American community and society at large, where vulnerability and mutual support are recognized as valuable. This shift could transform personal relationships, breaking down stereotypes and opening up healthier, more supportive connections for everyone.

What Do Most Men Say They Need From A Relationship With A Woman?

It's just as important for women to understand what men need in a relationship. Life goes both ways—knowing what men look for can help keep expectations in check, even as you stick to your own boundaries. To create a balanced relationship, it's essential to consider what men value from their partners.

In most relationships, men appreciate certain things that build a strong, lasting connection. Support, acceptance, appreciation, and companionship are often at the top of the list, each one key to keeping the relationship healthy and sustainable.

Support is especially valued by men. It's not just about helping with day-to-day tasks; emotional support makes a big difference. Men deeply value a partner who gets where they're coming from and stands by them. When a woman understands his dreams, career goals, and the pressures he's dealing with, and offers encouragement through tough times, it means a lot. This kind of support reassures him that he's not tackling life's battles alone and that he has a partner who believes in his potential.

For many men, acceptance in a relationship is non-negotiable. We want to feel accepted just as we are—flaws, quirks, and all—without feeling like we need to change to fit someone else's idea of who we should be. When a man feels truly accepted, he can be himself without pretense, which is essential for building genuine, deep emotional connections.

Then there's appreciation, which is big for us. Men need to feel valued for all they bring to the table, whether that's financially, emotionally, or through the little and big things done to keep the relationship and home running smoothly. Small gestures of gratitude go a long way—they show a man his efforts are noticed and remind him he's valued. When appreciated, he'll naturally want to give more, putting in the work to see the relationship thrive.

And finally, companionship ties it all together. Men often look for a partner who's also a friend, someone who shares similar interests and genuinely enjoys spending time together. Whether it's bonding over hobbies, watching a good film, or having real conversations, men value a partner who can be both a friend and a lover. This balance adds joy to daily life and strengthens the emotional bond that keeps the relationship steady.

Understanding the Unique Needs of African American Men in Relationships

For African American men, relationship needs like support, acceptance, appreciation, and companionship are pretty universal. But there's a layer of depth that comes from lived experiences shaped by culture, history, and society's expectations. These unique factors play a big role in what we look for and need in a relationship.

Support isn't just a simple word for African American men—it's a pillar. And often, it means something deeper: having a partner who recognizes the unique stress that racial dynamics can bring. Emotional support from someone who understands the weight of racial identity and the challenges of navigating systemic issues is invaluable. A partner who "gets it" can offer strength, helping him face these daily realities. This kind of understanding builds a strong bond based on trust and mutual respect, creating a space where he can feel fully seen and supported.

Acceptance is huge, especially in a world that often wants to put African American men into narrow boxes. Having a partner who sees past stereotypes and allows him to just be is powerful. It's about being valued for his individuality—without the need to fit into someone else's ideas of what a Black man should be or how masculinity should look. This level of acceptance means he doesn't have to wear any masks; he can be genuine, free from the pressures of society's labels, in a space that respects his unique identity.

Appreciation for African American men means recognizing the often-overlooked efforts they put into their roles within the family and community, especially as they work through added challenges. When a man's resilience, strength, and integrity as a provider are acknowledged, despite the extra weight he often carries, it's incredibly affirming. Feeling seen for his dedication reinforces his value and role in the family and strengthens the bond.

Companionship is also vital, and for many African American men, it's made richer by shared cultural experiences and understandings. Bonding over cultural practices, shared histories, and providing strength through unique challenges adds layers to the connection. This kind of companionship goes beyond the surface; it creates a deeper partnership rooted in a common experience and mutual respect.

Open communication is critical too. With the pressures and demands Black men often face in the outside world, having a partner who offers a safe space for open conversation—where he can be vulnerable without fear or judgment—is invaluable. When he can trust that he'll be heard and supported, it builds a relationship of mutual trust and understanding, enabling both partners to stand strong against personal and societal challenges together.

These needs aren't just preferences; they're deeply tied to cultural identity. A relationship that respects and nurtures a man's cultural background is stronger and more connected, grounded in mutual respect and a shared understanding of what it means to navigate the world as an African American man. This kind of relationship builds a bond that's not only personal but also rooted in understanding and honoring his unique experiences.

Signs your Relationship is Stuck

Identifying whether a relationship is stagnating and lacks a plan for the future can be crucial for a woman who wants to ensure her emotional investment is leading toward a meaningful and mutually fulfilling partnership. Here are some signs that might indicate a relationship is stuck with no plans for the future:

1. **Lack of Future Discussions:** If discussions about the future are consistently avoided, dismissed, or met with vague responses by your partner, it could be a sign that they are not considering a long-term commitment. A partner interested in the future will be open to discussing and planning for upcoming life events, goals, and milestones.

2. **No Progression in Commitment:** If the relationship seems to be in a constant state of "dating" without any progression towards more significant commitment milestones (e.g., moving in together, engagement, marriage, or planning a family), this could

indicate a lack of intention or desire to move the relationship forward.

3. **Avoidance of Serious Topics:** If your partner consistently avoids severe conversations about the relationship, financial planning, career moves that involve each other, or any other decisions that would require joint planning, it might suggest they are not envisioning a future together.

4. **Absence of Mutual Goals:** In a healthy relationship aiming for a long-term future, couples often have shared goals, whether they're financial, lifestyle-related, or personal aspirations that involve each other. A lack of shared visions can indicate that the relationship lacks depth and long-term expectations.

5. **Lack of Inclusion in Personal Life:** If you notice that you are not included in significant aspects of your partner's life, such as family gatherings, special events, or even daily routines, this could indicate a reluctance to integrate lives more deeply.

6. **Inconsistent or Uncertain Communication:** Communication is the lifeline of progressing relationships. Suppose interactions become inconsistent or your partner often seems uncertain about making plans, even in the short term. In that case, it might be a sign that they are not prioritizing the relationship.

7. **Unwillingness to Resolve Conflicts:** Every relationship encounters conflicts, but a partner invested in the future will want to resolve disputes and ensure both parties are happy. Avoidance of resolving

conflicts can indicate a lack of interest in improving or deepening the relationship.

8. **No Interest in Your Personal Growth:** A partner who sees a future with you will support your personal and professional growth. A lack of interest in your achievements or ambitions can be a red flag that they are not looking at the relationship as a long-term partnership.

9. **Feeling Stagnant or Unfulfilled:** Sometimes, the most telling sign is your feelings about the relationship. Suppose you feel that the relationship is not growing and you are not fulfilling your personal or couple's goals. In that case, it might be time to evaluate if this relationship has a future.

Recognizing these signs can help a woman determine whether her relationship has a stagnant nature with no future plans or if there are areas that she and her partner can work on together to align their visions and expectations.

CHAPTER 7

Just Because I Want It Doesn't Mean It's Good for Me

Strong attraction or intense passion in a relationship can be confused with being genuinely compatible with someone. Just because a relationship feels exciting initially doesn't mean it will benefit you long-term.

First, it's important to understand that intense attraction is often about the thrill and excitement of a new relationship. These feelings are strong, but they don't always last. Compatibility, on the other hand, is about how well you get along with someone over time. It includes sharing similar values, having mutual respect, and supporting each other's goals in life.

To tell the difference between just feeling good and actually being good for each other, ask yourself a few questions:

Do we share the same values and beliefs?

When considering if you and your partner share the same values and beliefs, you're looking at the core aspects that define each of you. This alignment can be crucial for long-term compatibility in a relationship. Here's a more detailed look at why these matters and how to assess it:

Understanding Values and Beliefs: Values are the principles that guide how we live and make decisions.

They might include views on honesty, work ethic, family, or how to handle money. Beliefs are often tied to our views on religion, politics, or what we think about the roles in relationships. Both values and beliefs shape our expectations in life and relationships.

Why They Matter: Sharing similar values and beliefs can lead to a smoother relationship because you are likely to agree on handling life's big questions and decisions. For example, if you both value family highly, you're likely to prioritize spending time with family or planning for your family's future. Or, if you share a belief in the importance of honesty, you'll both prioritize transparency and trust.

Potential Conflicts: Differences in values and beliefs can lead to conflicts. Suppose one partner values independence and the other values close companionship. In that case, they might clash over how much time to spend together versus apart. Similarly, suppose one partner has strong religious beliefs, and the other doesn't. In that case, it might lead to disagreements on celebrating holidays, raising children, or making ethical decisions.

Assessing Your Compatibility: To find out if you share values and beliefs, you can:

- Discuss life goals and what each of you envisions for your future.
- Discuss how you handle finances, work, and leisure to see if your lifestyles and priorities align.

- Share your thoughts on family roles, children, and how to handle conflicts.
- Observe how each of you acts in various situations. Actions often reveal actual values and beliefs more than words.

Navigating Differences: It's possible to have a healthy relationship despite some differences in values and beliefs as long as there is respect for each other's viewpoints and a willingness to find common ground or compromise when needed.

In essence, exploring whether you share the same values and beliefs is about understanding if you can fundamentally agree on essential aspects of life and support each other in ways that matter most. This understanding can significantly influence the depth and durability of your relationship.

Can we talk openly about our feelings and problems?

Talking openly about feelings and problems is critical to any healthy relationship. This goes beyond simply sharing thoughts; it's about feeling safe and respected when expressing emotions, whether positive or negative.

Why Open Communication Matters: Open communication is essential because it builds trust and strengthens the bond between partners. Discussing your feelings and problems without fear of judgment or retaliation creates a supportive environment that fosters intimacy and understanding. This openness helps prevent misunderstandings and the buildup of resentment when issues are left unaddressed.

Assessing Your Communication: Consider several factors to determine if you and your partner effectively communicate openly. Consider your comfort level: Do you feel at ease discussing your worries, fears, and joys with your partner? Reflect on their responses when you share your feelings. Do they listen attentively and offer empathy, or do they become defensive and dismissive? Lastly, consider the outcomes of your discussions. Do they generally lead to some resolution or mutual understanding, or do they tend to end in arguments without any resolution?

Improving Communication: If open communication is lacking, there are ways to improve it. Start by practicing active listening, which entirely concentrates on what your partner is saying without planning your following response. Show that you are engaged with nods or verbal affirmations. Also, create opportunities for deeper conversations by asking open-ended questions about how your partner feels about different aspects of your life together. When discussing sensitive topics, approach them calmly and respectfully. Use "I" statements to express your feelings without accusing or blaming your partner—for example, saying "I feel upset when..." instead of "You always make me feel..."

Establish Ground Rules: Agree on rules for handling difficult conversations, such as taking a break if emotions become too intense and avoiding derogatory remarks or name-calling.

Dealing with Challenges: Not every conversation will be straightforward, especially when it involves personal issues or significant disagreements. Suppose communication remains a challenge despite your efforts. In that case, seeking guidance from a counselor or therapist who can facilitate better communication might be helpful.

By working to create an environment where both partners feel safe expressing their feelings and discussing their problems openly, you lay the foundation for a more substantial and enduring relationship. This approach resolves immediate issues and equips you both with the skills necessary to tackle future challenges together.

Do we support each other's dreams and goals?

Supporting each other's dreams and goals is vital in a healthy relationship because it shows that you value and respect each other's aspirations and life ambitions. Feeling supported fosters, a sense of partnership and shared journey, which is crucial for long-term satisfaction and happiness.

Understanding Mutual Support: Mutual support in a relationship means more than just encouraging during a tough time or celebrating each other's successes. It involves actively listening to your partner's dreams and aspirations, understanding their needs to achieve these goals, and offering practical and emotional support. This could be anything from providing constructive feedback on their ideas to helping them network with potential contacts or simply being a sounding board for their thoughts and frustrations.

Assessing Support: To evaluate how well you support each other's dreams and goals, reflect on how much you know about your partner's aspirations. Consider whether you make time to discuss these aspirations and whether you take them seriously. Consider how often you ask about their progress and offer help or encouragement. It's also important to notice if there's balance between both of you and get equal opportunities to pursue individual goals while maintaining your relationship?

Encouraging Each Other: Encouraging each other's goals isn't just about verbal affirmations; it's also about making sacrifices and compromises. For example, one partner might take on more household responsibilities to give the other time to study for a course or work on a project. It could also mean relocating to support a partner's career opportunity or agreeing to budget adjustments to finance a partner's startup business.

Handling Challenges: Supporting each other's dreams does not mean you won't face challenges. Different ambitions can sometimes pull partners in opposite directions, straining the relationship. In such cases, it's crucial to communicate openly and honestly about your feelings and to negotiate compromises that respect both partners' aspirations. This might mean alternating focus between each person's goals or finding a new dream that you can pursue together.

Supporting each other's dreams and goals creates a nurturing environment for individual growth, essential for a healthy, thriving relationship. It shows commitment to each other's happiness and success, which can strengthen the bond between partners.

Are we comfortable with ourselves when we're together?

Feeling comfortable and being oneself in a relationship clearly indicates a healthy partnership. This comfort level allows both individuals to express their true selves without fear of judgment or criticism, fostering trust and intimacy.

When partners are comfortable around each other, they feel free to share their thoughts, feelings, and experiences openly. This openness is crucial for building a solid foundation in any relationship. It means being able to laugh together, share silence without discomfort, and express vulnerabilities without fearing negative consequences. Comfort in a relationship also means accepting each other's quirks and habits, acknowledging that no one is perfect and that these unique traits contribute to each person's individuality.

Assessing this comfort can be straightforward. Consider whether you can spend long periods in silence without filling the air with small talk. Think about how you act when you're together; do you dress or behave in a way that isn't true to who you are because you want to impress your partner, or are you relaxed and natural? Also, reflect on how you communicate. Can you discuss complex topics and express when something bothers you, or do you hold back your true feelings to keep the peace?

Being comfortable and authentic with your partner also means you can manage conflicts constructively. In a cozy relationship, conflicts are less about winning and more about understanding and resolving differences. This doesn't mean you'll never get upset with each other, but rather that when disagreements occur, you're both committed to resolving them in ways that are respectful and considerate of each other's feelings.

Overall, the ability to be yourself with your partner is one of the most telling signs of a healthy relationship. It allows both individuals to grow and evolve together, knowing they have the support and acceptance of their partner in their most authentic form. This level of comfort and openness ultimately deepens the connection between partners, making the relationship resilient and fulfilling.

Answering these questions can help you figure out if the relationship is just exciting for now or if it has the potential to be a healthy, long-lasting partnership. Remember, what feels good right now might not necessarily be what's best for you in the long run.

CHAPTER 8

Negotiating Non-Negotiables

Negotiating non-negotiables in a relationship might seem paradoxical since non-negotiables are, by definition, aspects or values an individual is unwilling to compromise on. These include fundamental beliefs, life goals, personal boundaries, and core values. Addressing these issues is crucial to ensuring both partners feel respected and fulfilled.

The process begins with clear communication. Both partners must openly discuss their non-negotiables early in the relationship to understand and evaluate each other's boundaries and expectations. This dialogue is about stating what you are unwilling to compromise on and understanding why certain things are crucial to your partner. This level of understanding is pivotal for building empathy and respect, even without a shared stance.

So non-negotiables in a relationship is about protecting your peace and making sure you're respected at all times. It starts with knowing what you stand for and what you won't tolerate. A woman has to take a hard look at her values, her past, and what she needs to feel safe and supported. For example, if honesty is important, she has to make it clear from the jump that lies and half-truths won't fly. It's about being real with yourself first, so you can be real with anyone else who comes into your life.

Once she knows her limits, she has to put them into words. **Communication is key—she can't assume someone will just pick up on what she needs. Whether it's about time, respect, or trust, she has to say it plain.** For instance, if she values quality time, she might say, "I need us to have a set time every week where it's just us—no phones, no distractions, just us connecting." When she lays it out clearly, there's no room for misunderstanding, and it sets the tone for how she expects to be treated.

Physical boundaries are another layer of self-respect. She's got to be upfront about what she's comfortable with, whether it's personal space or how quickly things progress. If she's not ready for intimacy, she can say, "I need more time to feel comfortable before we take this to a deeper level." Emotional boundaries are just as important because not everyone deserves access to her heart. If someone's dismissing her feelings, she has to check that and say, "When I share how I feel, I need you to listen and respect it. If that's not happening, we've got a problem."

Then there's the money talk and the time talk. Mixing finances can get tricky, so it's smart to make that clear early on. She might say, "For now, I think we should keep our finances separate until we're further along." On the flip side, time is just as valuable. A woman who knows her worth isn't about to let anyone monopolize her time. She might say, "I value my time with you, but I also need space for my own goals, my friends, and my family. Let's make time for each other while still respecting our individual lives."

In this digital age, even social media needs boundaries. **Not everyone needs to know every detail of the relationship, and she can let that be known:** "I'd rather keep our relationship private for now and focus on us, not the outside noise." If someone crosses her boundaries—whether it's canceling plans at the last minute or disrespecting her values—she has to call it out. For example, if someone keeps making her feel like an afterthought, she could say, "I need you to show me I'm a priority. If that's not happening, we need to reevaluate this."

And let's be real, she's got to keep an eye out for red flags. If her boundaries are ignored over and over, it's time to step back. She might say, "I've been clear about what I need, and it's not being respected. I won't keep repeating myself." Knowing when to walk away is a power move—it's not giving up, it's choosing herself.

Finally, self-awareness and self-care are the foundation of keeping those boundaries strong. Checking in with herself regularly, whether through prayer, journaling, or talking to someone she trusts, keeps her grounded. When she knows her worth and enforces her limits, she's not just protecting herself— she's building the kind of relationship that's rooted in mutual respect and love. A woman who sets boundaries isn't just surviving—she's thriving.

When non-negotiables clash, it's essential to assess the overall compatibility of the relationship. Are these non-negotiables consistently hindering the relationship, or can mutual respect prevail without complete agreement. For instance, if one partner desires children and the other adamantly does not, this difference in life goals might be irreconcilable. However, differences in less critical preferences, such as hobbies or taste in music, can often be respected without agreement.

Finding creative compromises is key when non-negotiables create tension but are not diametrically opposed. This doesn't mean altering your non-negotiables but finding ways to respect each other's needs through adjustments in behaviors or expectations. For example, if one partner needs significant personal space, scheduling regular times for each person to have time alone may satisfy this need without making the other partner feel neglected.

Seeking external guidance from a counselor or therapist can be beneficial when non-negotiables cause significant conflict. Professional help can offer new perspectives and mediation strategies that help both partners better understand each other's positions and explore potential solutions that respect both individuals' non-negotiables.

Ultimately, the successful navigation of non-negotiables in a relationship hinges on mutual respect, effective communication, and a willingness to understand each other's deepest needs and boundaries. The ties can accommodate non-negotiables with foundational solid elements without requiring either partner to compromise their core values and beliefs.

CHAPTER 9

Breaking Deal Breakers

I gnoring established deal breakers in relationships can have significant long-term consequences that undermine personal integrity and self-respect. Deal breakers are essentially boundaries set to protect one's well-being and values, indicating unacceptable aspects or behaviors in a relationship. When these boundaries are overlooked, it can lead to a relationship filled with resentment, mistrust, and emotional turmoil.

Firstly, when you compromise on your deal breakers, you might start justifying behaviors you previously determined unacceptable. This could be anything from disrespect to differing views on fundamental life choices like having children or marriage. Rationalizing such behaviors can create a cycle where you continue to lower your standards and simply accept more than what is healthy for you to maintain the relationship. This often leads to a significant decrease in self-esteem as you question your worth and values.

Moreover, ignoring deal breakers can also impact mental and emotional health. Staying in a relationship that fundamentally disagrees with your core beliefs and boundaries can lead to ongoing stress and anxiety. The constant strain of reconciling your true desires with the reality of your relationship can create a persistent state of discomfort and dissatisfaction. This stress can manifest physically, leading to symptoms like sleeplessness, loss of appetite, or even more severe health issues over time.

Maintaining integrity and self-respect in relationships is essential to honoring your deal breakers. This involves having clear, open conversations about your boundaries early in the relationship. It's necessary to be straightforward about what you can and cannot accept from a partner. If a boundary is crossed, it is crucial to address it immediately rather than allowing resentment to build. This might require difficult conversations or the willingness to leave a relationship that does not meet your fundamental needs.

To navigate these challenges effectively, it's helpful to remain connected to your values and regularly reflect on whether your relationship aligns with them. Support from friends, family, or a therapist can also be invaluable in maintaining perspective and reinforcing your commitment to your own well-being.

Ultimately, respecting your deal breakers isn't just about maintaining personal integrity; it's also about ensuring that your relationships are genuinely supportive and enriching. While ending a relationship or addressing significant issues may be challenging, doing so is often necessary to ensure your long-term happiness and health.

A Man Leading With Money

Leading with money is a common tactic among influential individuals, often used as a shortcut to gain attention and affection. This approach, however, can obscure genuine connections, as it places financial wealth at the forefront of interactions, leaving little room for more substantive qualities to shine through. Men who lead with their wallets might feel that their financial clout can buy them anything, including relationships, but this often leads to a lack of meaningful personal boundaries.

Consider a hypothetical man of wealth—someone with millions to spare. For him, money is no object when impressing a potential partner. Flying someone to the French Riviera or Dubai for a date might seem extravagant to most. Still, to him, it's just another transaction. The ease with which he can offer these experiences can often overshadow the need to develop a deeper, more personal connection. What's $10,000 to a millionaire? Practically nothing, but for a relationship grounded on such gestures, the emotional investment might be just as insubstantial.

For women, it can be enticing to accept these grand gestures. The glamour of luxury and the allure of a seemingly carefree lifestyle can be compelling. Yet, just because the setting is lavish doesn't mean the relationship provides the substance or intimacy necessary for long-term connection. Enjoying a good time doesn't equate to a meaningful alone time where actual bonds are formed.

Thus, the boundary that needs to be established is not just by the woman, to not be swayed solely by material generosity, but crucially by the man. Men in these positions must learn to set boundaries on how much they allow their wealth to lead their relationships. It's about balancing generosity and genuine connection, ensuring their financial status enhances rather than defining their relationships. The right one for anyone, regardless of their bank account, should be someone who values emotional and intellectual connections beyond financial ones.

A man with substantial wealth might not hesitate to spend $10,000 on a luxurious weekend or lavish you with a thousand-dollar dinner. For someone with deep pockets, such expenditures are trivial, a mere drop in the bucket. It's a dynamic seen among the affluent, where financial generosity can sometimes substitute for deeper, more meaningful forms of companionship. Take the example of a high-profile individual like a celebrity, who might be seen with a new companion every month, each one receiving what could be dubbed a "starter kit" of high-end fashion items—Louis Vuitton and Gucci purses or a pair of red-bottomed shoes, even a sports car. These are impressive gifts, but they're also impersonal, purchased as quickly as one might order a drink at a bar.

For women, this scenario poses a crucial question about discerning the true intentions of a wealthy suitor. Is this man genuinely interested in you as a person, or is he simply filling a void with your presence, using his wealth to keep you at his side? It's flattering to receive such attention and gifts, especially those you might never have afforded yourself. However, it's essential to recognize the signs of a fundamentally transactional relationship.

You might find that this man only spends time with you on his terms and schedule. Perhaps you feel like you're just part of a rotation, always available at his convenience but never indeed prioritized. The red flags might be obscured by the dazzle of luxury, making it difficult to see that this relationship lacks substance. He's not investing time or emotional energy; he's investing money. And while the material goods are tangible and immediate, they don't foster a genuine or sustainable connection.

Understanding these dynamics is crucial for anyone navigating a relationship with a wealthy individual who leads with their wallet. It's about looking beyond the surface glamour to the interactions that define your connection. Are you valued beyond what is spent on you? Are your conversations as rich as the dinners he can afford? Recognizing these signs can help you determine whether you're with someone who sees you as a partner or an accessory to their lifestyle.

When someone has not experienced certain luxuries before, it's easy to be dazzled by gestures that seem generous but may actually lack sincerity. This can be particularly true when someone uses wealth as a facade, obscuring deeper issues like disrespect or indifference towards you. Such a person leads with their money, mistaking financial expenditure for emotional investment, and often fails to genuinely consider the needs and values of the person they are dating.

Consider the story of a woman who grew up accustomed to luxury, thanks to her family's wealth. She went on a date with a man who spent the evening boasting about his Mercedes, evidently trying to impress her. However, she was unimpressed; she had been around such luxury all her life and even owned a brand-new Audi. To her, his attempt to impress with material possessions came off as shallow and misplaced—he didn't understand his audience. It turned her off not because she wasn't impressed by wealth but because he was clearly leading with his money rather than showing genuine interest or compatibility. He missed an opportunity to connect on a deeper, more personal level, choosing instead to showcase his assets.

This scenario illustrates that having money and being willing to spend it doesn't necessarily equate to caring or understanding. It's a common trap for those not used to wealth to see lavish spending as a sign of genuine interest or affection. However, this isn't always the case. The right partner understands and values you beyond what they can buy. They invest in getting to know you, your interests, and your dreams, not just in impressing you with their wealth.

A man might have the means to give you anything you want. Still, suppose his approach to dating is primarily through financial gestures. In that case, it's crucial to question whether his interest is in you as a person or merely in how he can use his wealth to keep you interested. Sometimes, a man with less money who invests more thoughtfully and personally into the relationship can demonstrate a deeper care than one who can afford to spend extravagantly but does so without real attachment. Thus, discerning genuine care from monetary allure is critical in navigating relationships, especially when money is involved.

So, which one is the right one, and which one is the wrong one? Is it the man with money who cares about you or who may have less but still cares deeply? In today's era, dominated by social media and podcasts, there's a lot of focus on what people earn. The quest for a "six-figure man" equates wealth with the right partner. However, men with substantial incomes often want to control the relationship, motivated by their financial clout. If you don't match their wealth or are not contributing equally, you might ask: why would they value your decisions or seek your advice?

Many wealthy men enjoy dominating the dynamics of a relationship, intent on maintaining control. On the other hand, a man who earns less might be more inclined to foster an equal partnership, which many women unfortunately overlook in their pursuit of a wealthier partner. But having six figures doesn't guarantee he can provide love, respect, or genuine care. Wealth may bring power, but power doesn't necessarily get the right attributes to a relationship.

So, does a six-figure income ensure that he is the right one? Can he love you, care for you, and respect you, not just with his wallet but with his actions and heart? Wealth alone isn't a reliable indicator of a suitable partner. True compatibility involves more than financial provision; it requires emotional investment and mutual respect, elements no amount of money can buy.

Indeed, financial status does not necessarily dictate a person's inclination to control a relationship. Sometimes, a man with fewer economic resources might attempt to exert control over a woman who also may not have much. However, holding firm to your standards and desires in relationships is essential.

On my podcast, I often emphasize to women: **do not lower your expectations or settle for less than what you truly want.** I firmly believe that women should strive for what they desire in a partner. Yes, it may take longer to find a man who has the financial stability you want and respects and loves you deeply—someone who views you as an equal partner.

Especially for women who might feel they don't have much going for themselves, it's crucial to remember that you deserve a partner who brings more to the table than just material wealth. It's about finding someone who can genuinely appreciate and include you in every aspect of life, especially if you have children.

The wrong partner is often overly focused on themselves or their perspectives, neglecting to include you and your needs. They talk about what's relevant to them without considering your input. For a woman with children, it's vital to find a partner who naturally incorporates concern for your children into the relationship, showing genuine interest and care without needing to prompt it.

Indeed, finding a partner who respects and loves you and meets your financial expectations can be a journey that requires patience and discernment. It's essential not to settle for less, especially with someone who fails to fully recognize or integrate crucial aspects of your life, such as your children. This commitment to waiting for the right partner, one who genuinely aligns with your life and values, is crucial for long-term happiness.

CHAPTER 10

Crossing Boundaries

Relationships are profound lessons, teaching us about ourselves and how we interact with others. We can draw valuable insights from every relationship that doesn't work out and develop more precise boundaries. It's akin to undergoing an exit interview at the end of a job—reflecting on what went well, what didn't, and why it didn't work. This reflective process requires a particular maturity, acknowledging the other person's contributions and your role in the outcome.

For example, consider being married for 20 years to a wonderful husband. Even though the marriage ends, you can still maintain a friendship and respect for each other. Engaging in what could be likened to an "exit interview" with the help of a counselor can be incredibly beneficial. It helps explore why your paths diverged and is essential for understanding the boundaries that must be established for future relationships based on the lessons learned from past ones.

For those curious about what an exit interview entails, here's a detailed explanation: In the aftermath of a divorce, this novel concept, borrowed from the corporate world and adapted to personal relationships, involves a candid, structured discussion about experiences and potential improvements. When applied to a divorce, this practice transforms into a tool for emotional closure and mutual understanding between former spouses. This not only aids in healing but also in moving forward with newfound clarity and insight.

Picture two individuals who once pledged the deepest of vows, now seated across from one another, potentially for the last occasion in such an intimate setting. They engage in a thoughtful dialogue about their shared history. This conversation isn't about re-igniting lost love or unearthing old grievances; it's a pursuit of understanding. They explore the dynamics that once bonded them and the strains that ultimately drove them apart, embracing a moment meant for reflection rather than blame.

An exit interview following a divorce provides a platform for both individuals to articulate any unre-solved emotions and thoughts that remained unexpressed amid the turmoil of separation. This dialogue requires substantial maturity and emotional stability as it navigates the fine line between candor and empathy. It seeks to comprehend how two lives, once intricately woven together, can respectfully and supportively diverge.

For many, this process's actual value lies in its closure. It acts as a formal conclusion, akin to the end of a profound book, allowing both parties to collectively summarize their shared chapter before turning the page. Additionally, there's immense potential for personal growth. Both individuals can unearth crucial lessons about themselves and their relational dynamics by dissecting what succeeded and faltered. Such introspection is invaluable, potentially guiding them toward forming healthier relationships in the future.

When children are part of the equation, maintaining a friendly relationship post-divorce isn't just advantageous; it's imperative. An exit interview can establish a framework for future interactions, particularly around co-parenting and mutual respect, helping each parent align on the best ways to support their children from separate homes.

Nonetheless, the practicality of such an interview dramatically depends on the circumstances surrounding the breakup. A calm and reflective discussion may not be feasible in situations marked by deep wounds, betrayal, or intense conflict. In these cases, the involvement of a mediator or therapist might be crucial to safely and constructively navigating the emotional terrain.

Ultimately, the exit interview serves as a bridge from the past to the future. It offers a chance to transform pain and misunderstanding into wisdom and personal growth. While not all relationships may conclude with such clarity and maturity, for those that do, the exit interview stands as a poignant affirmation of the enduring human capacity for understanding and transformation.

Boundaries act as the concrete lessons drawn from our experiences, shaping lines that should not be crossed. These guidelines help safeguard our well-being and ensure our relationships progress healthily and respectfully. Consider a simple yet impactful boundary: deciding not to go on a date until communicating with the person for two weeks over the phone. This boundary, though straightforward, plays a crucial role in setting the pace and nature of the interaction.

For a practical illustration, I recall interviewing a couple on the streets of Atlanta for a segment titled "When the Wrong One Comes." They had only just met moments before I approached them. In clearly displaying her boundaries, the woman had given the man her Instagram page rather than her phone number. She explained that she doesn't share her number until she feels comfortable. This boundary, set during the early stages of a new acquaintance, is a testament to the modern dynamics of dating. In the digital era, platforms like Facebook, Instagram, and TikTok have become standard starting points for communication. By setting such a boundary, she maintains control over her interactions, advancing to more personal levels only when she feels secure— a strategic move circumvents the potential need to block unwanted advances later on.

Once identified and firmly established, these boundaries serve as personal guidelines and protectors as we navigate relationships. They are not merely about exclusion but are rooted in self-respect and the assurance that anyone who enters our lives will honor these clearly defined lines.

Boundaries are the essential safeguards we establish in our lives, formed in the aftermath of experiences, particularly from relationships that have left scars. They are our firm declarations of "I don't like this, so I'm putting this up" or "You can't go further until I say so." Setting boundaries is everyone's prerogative; crucially, they help us weed out incompatible partners.

Boundaries emerge from the ashes of relationships that didn't pan out; they are the sum of our painful lessons. They teach us what we do not like and how we might have moved too fast or made missteps. There's a well-known saying about insanity: doing the same thing repeatedly and expecting different results. In the context of personal growth, if repeated behaviors lead to pain, then it's wise to set boundaries to prevent these patterns.

Take, for example, the boundaries one might set around intimacy. For some, it might be not engaging in sexual activities until marriage, or perhaps waiting 90 days, or even until a proposal is made. If past experiences have shown that moving too quickly into physical intimacy leads to heartbreak, setting a boundary like "not until marriage" or "not until I'm truly valued" becomes a protective measure to avoid repeating past mistakes.

It's important to note that boundaries aren't always innate; they are often forged through the fires of our missteps and heartaches. Most of us learn to set boundaries only after we've felt the sting of their absence. Therefore, I encourage you, the reader, to reflect on your experiences as you progress through this book. Take the time to establish boundaries that honor your values and ensure your emotional and physical well-being. By setting these boundaries, you assert control over your personal space and emotional health, guiding future relationships toward more fulfilling and respectful interactions.

Boundaries are not up for negotiation. With billions of people worldwide, it's illogical to compromise the standards that protect your personal well-being. This is precisely why non-negotiables are called non-negotiables—they are fundamental principles that should not be altered to accommodate someone else. This effort to force compatibility is often why we end up hurt. Why attempt to force a fit if you've spotted a red flag?

Boundaries need to be taken seriously. They aren't merely suggestions but firm lines that should not be crossed. Attempting to change someone to fit into your predefined boundaries is impractical. It contradicts the purpose of setting them in the first place. I firmly believe that while adjustments in behaviors might be possible, fundamentally changing a person is not—and should not be—the goal.

Moreover, if I need to explicitly state my boundaries, it might prevent me from seeing someone's true nature. If you are genuinely incompatible with someone, they might initially try to conform to your expectations, acting as a chameleon to blend into your life seamlessly. But this is just a temporary facade. Eventually, their true colors will show. A person who alters themselves extensively to fit into what you want is likely not in the relationship for the right reasons. They are the 'wrong one'—someone who temporarily morphs to meet your criteria, driven by motives that don't align with genuine partnership.

This concept underscores the significance of maintaining one's boundaries silently at times. You allow others to reveal their true selves by not declaring all your boundaries. This strategy helps identify who is genuinely compatible with you and who is merely pretending, ensuring that you foster relationships authentically aligned with your core values.

Boundaries need to be unequivocal and immutable. Knowing your boundaries internally is crucial, but how you communicate them can also be tactful yet firm. Instead of labeling every rule as a boundary, state your stance clearly. For example, suppose you're not engaging in sex before marriage or are waiting for a certain period. In that case, you don't need to declare, "This is my boundary." Instead, you might say, "I'm not having sex before marriage." This approach clearly communicates your position without framing it as a negotiation.

Suppose someone responds with desires that conflict with your boundaries, such as wanting immediate intimacy. It's perfectly acceptable to politely disengage, "It was nice meeting you, but I don't think we're looking for the same things." This stance underscores a critical point: you must not be afraid to walk away from someone who isn't right for you. There is a common fear of loneliness or the belief that no one else will come along, but compromising your boundaries is not the solution. Remaining firm in your boundaries protects your integrity. It ensures you do not lose yourself in trying to become something you're not or doing things that aren't true to your values.

To illustrate this with a personal anecdote—and you can use this example as it suits your needs— A well-known celebrity experienced something similar. She met a young woman in Los Angeles, where the cannabis industry is prominent. Even though she never smoked and disliked all forms of smoke, she found herself compromising her boundaries because she was enamored and moved too quickly into the relationship without truly knowing him on a deeper level. This compromise on something fundamental to her beliefs was a mistake. It's a clear example of why boundaries should be firm and non-negotiable. Even in love, one must adhere to one's core values or risk losing oneself entirely.

In relationships, boundaries are not just lines we draw; they are declarations of our core values and deal-breakers. Take, for instance, the story of a woman who, despite her status as a Christian celebrity, found herself in a relationship with a smoker. This wasn't merely about disliking smoking; it conflicted with her personal and public values. Initially, she compromised, overlooking this significant incompatibility due to other redeeming qualities he might have had. However, her discomfort with his smoking persisted, and ultimately, despite his respect for her, she chose to end the relationship. This scenario illustrates a pivotal lesson: if a boundary is compromised, especially one tied closely to personal values, it often leads to dissatisfaction. You end up either living miserably with that compromise or walking away later, having wasted time and emotional energy on a relationship doomed from the start.

This story underscores the importance of recognizing when someone is not suitable for you sooner rather than later. Often, we attempt to force a fit, to make concessions that go against our fundamental nature, thinking we can change or that the other person will change. But just as a non-smoker might struggle to be with a smoker, so too might a workaholic find difficulty with someone who prioritizes leisure. I've experienced this firsthand; I love my work, and this passion is non-negotiable. It took several relationships and painful endings to realize that I needed a partner who understood and perhaps even shared my work ethic. This realization wasn't immediate but was honed through the experiences and missteps of past relationships.

Recognizing and adhering to your boundaries is not about being inflexible; it's about being honest with yourself and fair to others. Whether it's smoking, work habits, or any other fundamental aspect of your lifestyle, compromising on core issues rarely leads to a happy ending. Instead, it's about finding someone who naturally aligns with your life's rhythm and values, ensuring mutual satisfaction and respect within the relationship.

At some point, there should be a revelatory "aha" moment where it all clicks—you realize that boundaries and non-negotiables aren't just parallel concepts; they are intertwined. Discussing one invariably leads to the other because non-negotiables are the boundaries you absolutely refuse to compromise on. They're the lines you draw in the sand, saying, "This is not up for discussion."

So, let's address a common misconception directly: the notion that men always want sex and women don't. Let's dispel that myth right here in our conversation. Women do enjoy sex, but their approach often involves a desire for intimacy before physicality. They seek a connection that transcends the physical, including genuine dialogue and emotional closeness. It's not just about the act of sex itself;

it's about the context in which it occurs. Women often want to know that their partner can engage with them, standing up in conversation and life, not just lying down in the fleeting moments of intimacy.

This distinction is crucial because it speaks directly to non-negotiables in a relationship. Suppose intimacy and emotional connection are prerequisites for physical closeness. In that case, these are not just preferences but boundaries that define how the relationship must function. "I need to feel connected and valued beyond the physical aspect" is a powerful assertion of one's needs. It isn't a negotiation—it's stating a fundamental requirement for emotional and physical engagement. When these terms are laid out clearly, they help clear potential misunderstandings and align with a partner who respects and fulfills these essential needs.

Some women may find themselves at dinner, across from a man who possesses more than charm; he engages deeply with her intellect. Suppose he can genuinely listen and resonate with her thoughts and feelings. In that case, she might invite him for a nightcap without him having to broach the topic of intimacy. This scenario underscores a profound psychological truth: when a man connects with a woman on an intellectual and emotional level, he won't need to overtly seek physical intimacy—it becomes a natural progression of their interaction.

However, there's a significant contrast to someone who is not the right matching the wrong one. Suppose a man fails to engage a woman's mind and spirit. In that case, any advance feels disconnected, merely pursuing physical satisfaction. For her, the encounter remains superficial, perceived only as seeking sex, lacking the deeper connection she values. This distinction is crucial; it highlights the importance of intellectual and emotional intimacy in fostering a meaningful physical relationship. When these more profound layers of connection are missing, the physical aspect of the relationship can feel hollow and unsatisfying, underscoring the significance of aligning on more than just a surface level.

Intimacy isn't just about physical closeness; it's about emotional connection and intellectual engagement. A woman doesn't just want to communicate in the whispers of the night; she yearns for meaningful conversation outside the bedroom. It's about connection transcending the physical and being seen, heard, and understood.

The art of conversation is at the heart of true intimacy. When a man can engage a woman with genuine interest and articulate understanding, he doesn't just speak to her; he says into her life. That's the kind of interaction that can ignite a more profound desire within her. It's not about superficial chatter or flattery; it's about meaningful, engaging dialogue that resonates with her intellect and emotions.

But how do you foster such intimacy? It starts with truly being present and attentive. Today, many women feel that men struggle with this aspect of the relationship. Communication often falters not because men are incapable of it but perhaps because they've not been encouraged to express themselves in more expansive, emotional terms. Consider this typical scenario: a married man comes home and answers his wife's inquiry about his day with a brief "It was good."

Meanwhile, suppose you ask the woman about her day. In that case, she might unfold a narrative, expressing frustrations and highlighting with rich detail. This discrepancy in communication can sometimes lead to disconnecting.

For a woman, intimacy means that a man is genuinely interested in the granular details of her life—her challenges at work, the frustrating lunch encounter, or the call from daycare. It's about engaging in that story, showing empathy, and contributing to the conversation with monosyllabic responses and thoughtful dialogue. True intimacy involves diving deep into the other person's experience, validating their feelings, and sharing meaningful insights. When a man can communicate effectively and connect intellectually, he naturally makes a woman feel cherished and understood, paving the way for all dimensions of intimacy, including the physical.

Engaging deeply with a partner can dramatically shift the dynamic of a relationship, especially during challenging times. Imagine a scenario where a woman comes home after a hard day to share her struggles about potential layoffs or workplace stresses. A man who listens attentively can transform this moment into comfort and closeness. Instead of a nod, he might say, "Oh, come on, baby, lay on my chest," or "Let me run you a bath." These gestures of care and understanding can deepen the bond and pave the way for more intimate moments, not necessarily sexual but emotionally fulfilling.

Men often misunderstand that they can achieve a closer physical connection not just by initiating sex but by showing true intimacy throughout the day. Simple acts like sending thoughtful text messages, flowers, or even a small gesture like a lunch cash app can significantly impact. This isn't about grand gestures but consistent, small acts of kindness and attention that accumulate during the dating stage—well before marriage even enters the conversation.

However, the modern dating scene sometimes skews these attempts at intimacy. The trend of sending unsolicited photos of body parts via direct messages or social media is an example of where lines get crossed. Many women report receiving these kinds of images, which they find far from intimate or appealing. These actions don't engage a woman's mind or emotions; they fail to establish the intellectual and emotional connection many women seek.

It's crucial to understand that men and women experience attraction differently: men are typically stimulated by visual elements, while women are moved by what they hear and feel emotionally. Engaging a woman's mind and emotions, showing genuine interest in her thoughts and feelings, and listening intently can foster a deeper connection. It's about stimulating the intellect and touching the heart, not just sending digital images or focusing on physical attraction.

To cultivate a meaningful relationship, it's essential to communicate in ways that resonate emotionally and intellectually, understanding that intimacy is built on much more than physical interaction. This approach respects the boundaries important to a woman. It enriches the relationship, making it more likely to thrive and grow deeper.

Indeed, the ways men and women generally perceive attraction can vary significantly. Men are often described as more visual in their initial attractions; they might first notice physical attributes—their shape and features. It's not uncommon for a man to be drawn in by visual appeal, mentally sketching out his attraction before even a word is exchanged. This isn't to say men are superficial by nature. Still, visual cues often play a significant role in their initial interest.

Women, while they can also appreciate physical attractiveness, tend to weigh other qualities more heavily. They might acknowledge a man's appearance—"He has a nice smile"—but the substance beneath that smile often holds more significant sway. For many women, a meaningful conversation, a sense of humor, or intellectual compatibility sparks more profound interest. This divergence in attraction dynamics is not just anecdotal; it reflects broader psychological patterns observed across various cultures.

Consider an interaction I observed while interviewing a couple on the street. When asked what attracted him to her, the man immediately pointed to her physical appearance: "Look at her, ain't she fine?" Conversely, when the woman was asked the same question about him, she highlighted his conversational skills: "He had a good conversation." This not only underlines the visual versus verbal attraction divide but also showcases what often deepens interest for many women.

This phenomenon might explain why we sometimes see couples with a noticeable disparity in physical attractiveness. Passersby might wonder, "How did he get her?" The answer often lies not in the visual but in the verbal and emotional connection—the shared conversations, the mutual interests, and the emotional depth that has developed between them. These dynamic underscores the complexity of attraction and relationships, where physical appeal is just one layer of the intricate human experience of falling in love or forming partnerships.

How did he get her? It's a common question that might echo onlookers' minds when they see a couple where, superficially, the man might not match up to the woman's perceived level of attractiveness. The secret often lies not just in his ability to talk but in his ability to listen—an art that forms the core of authentic communication. It's not just about the words exchanged but how he attentively absorbs what she says, validating her thoughts and emotions.

When a woman says, "He sees me," she feels deeply understood. "Seeing" someone goes beyond mere physical observation—it's about perceiving who they genuinely are, recognizing their desires, fears, and dreams without them having to spell everything out. This phrase has evolved to mean a comprehensive, empathetic understanding. When a woman feels seen, she feels heard and valued, a robust basis for emotional intimacy.

This deep connection can draw a woman to a man despite any superficial "attractiveness" or social status discrepancies. However, a poignant twist often unfolds in relationships driven by physical chemistry without emotional depth. She might admit, "He's the wrong one, but the sex is good," which might compel her to stay longer than she should in an otherwise unfulfilling relationship. This situation illustrates a critical disconnect—good sex, while enjoyable, is not synonymous with a good relationship.

The allure of physical intimacy can sometimes cloud judgment, making it harder to acknowledge the lack of substantive communication and compatibility. Good sex does not compensate for poor communication; it doesn't build the foundation required for a lasting, meaningful relationship. The crucial question I often pose is: "Just because we can lie down together, does it mean we can stand up together?" Life isn't lived solely in the horizontal moments. True partnership is tested and displayed in standing, walking, and everyday living, which requires much more than physical compatibility.

Thus, distinguishing between the exhilaration of physical intimacy and the deeper fulfillment of emotional and intellectual connection is essential. The right partner can offer both—the one with whom you can share the silent moments and the conversations, the daily challenges and the joys, and standing strong together.

CONCLUSION

In conclusion, "When the Wrong One Comes" offers a path to empowerment and self-discovery for women working through relationships' ups and downs. Relationships can be complex and often challenging, but you don't have to feel lost. Focusing on critical aspects like education, patience, personal growth, therapy, and realistic expectations allows you to take charge of your emotional well-being and make choices that lead to a healthier and happier life.

One of the most powerful tools you can have is education. This doesn't only refer to formal schooling but also to learning about yourself, relationships, and how to set boundaries. When you invest time in reading, attending workshops, or seeking advice from mentors, you better understand what you truly want and deserve. Education helps you see the bigger picture and recognize good and bad patterns in your past relationships. With this knowledge, you become better equipped to make thoughtful decisions when choosing a partner. Instead of falling into the same traps, you can identify red flags early on and understand what behaviors align with your values and goals. Education allows you to make choices that align with your worth and future aspirations.

Patience is another essential ingredient in finding a fulfilling relationship. In a world that often demands instant gratification, patience allows you to slow down and look beyond the surface. It helps you gradually get to know someone, giving you time to observe how they treat you and others. More importantly, patience allows you to get to know yourself. It creates space for you to reflect on what you need in a partner and what truly makes you happy. By not rushing into relationships, you allow yourself to recognize whether a person aligns with your values and life goals. Patience also helps you heal from past relationships, allowing your heart to recover before you invest in someone new. This waiting time and reflection can prevent you from repeating old mistakes and help you approach new relationships with a clearer mind.

Personal growth is a lifelong journey that is significant in approaching love and relationships. As you grow, you better understand your strengths, weaknesses, desires, and fears. You become more confident and self-aware when you commit to improving yourself through reading, journaling, setting goals, or trying new hobbies. This growth helps you set boundaries that protect your peace and well-being. It also means you are less likely to settle for someone who doesn't treat you with the respect you deserve. Someone who has invested in their own growth understands that true happiness comes from within, not from another person. This makes you more likely to attract someone committed to self-improvement, creating the foundation for a healthier, more balanced relationship.

Seeking therapy can be a decisive step in your journey toward healing and understanding yourself better. Many of us carry wounds from past relationships, childhood experiences, or traumas that shape how we see ourselves and connect with others. Therapy offers a safe space to discuss these issues and gain new perspectives. A therapist can help you identify patterns in your behavior or thoughts that may be holding you back from forming a healthy relationship. They can also teach you coping mechanisms to deal with difficult emotions like anger, sadness, or anxiety. Therapy is about fixing what is broken and building a stronger, more resilient version of yourself. It equips you with the tools to navigate future relationship challenges without letting past hurt dictate your actions or choices. Investing in your mental health gives you the best chance of a fulfilling and emotionally balanced relationship.

Finally, maintaining level-headed expectations is crucial when it comes to love. Having dreams and desires for a relationship is natural, but it's important not to let those dreams cloud your judgment. Genuine relationships come with ups and downs, and no one is perfect. When you set your expectations too high, you might be constantly disappointed, overlooking a good partner simply because they don't match an idealized image. Being level-headed means appreciating the reality of relationships and the need for compromise, understanding, and growth together. It means recognizing that a healthy relationship is built over time, with effort from both sides. When you approach relationships with realistic expectations, you give yourself and your partner the grace to be human, allowing love to grow more authentically.

All of these elements—education, patience, personal growth, therapy, and realistic expectations—work together to help you navigate the challenges of relationships with wisdom and strength. By focusing on your journey and understanding what you need and deserve, you can make choices that bring you closer to healthy, fulfilling, and uplifting love. It's about taking control of your story and realizing that you are not defined by the wrong ones who have come into your life. Instead, you are determined by how you learn, heal, and grow from those experiences.

May this book serve as a guide and companion on your journey. I hope these pages' stories, insights, and advice have helped you see that you deserve a love that respects, cherishes, and uplifts you. Love should not be a source of pain or confusion but a partnership that brings out the best in you. Remember, the right person will never demand that you shrink or change who you are; they will appreciate your growth and walk alongside you as you become your best self.

As you move forward, be gentle with yourself. Take each step with courage, knowing that you are worthy of love and your journey is just as important as the destination. The right partner will come on time, but until then, your most important relationship is the one you have with yourself. Focus on nurturing that, and everything else will fall into place. Here's a future filled with self-love, confidence, and a love story that is truly deserving of the incredible person you are becoming.

ABOUT THE AUTHOR

Greg Davis . . . Pastor, Author, Speaker, and Television personality and Global Influencer, is one of the Founding Fathers of the Full Gospel Movement. Founded by Bishop Paul Morton Sr., now led by presiding Bishop Joseph W. Walker III. Although in ministry for 35 years, for the last 8 years, Greg Davis has successfully transitioned into relationships, being known as an experienced and trusted voice in all things dating, marriage, and relationships.

He brings a wealth of knowledge and 20 years of experience in marriage, making him an impactful relationship coach to all. As a single man of five years, he also provides relationship advice on his YouTube channel, "When The Wrong One Comes," and Instagram. Davis is also the author of over a dozen books, including one by the popular title "When The Wrong One Comes." Greg Davis has been in Media and television for over a decade, hosting numerous shows on The Word Network, the nation's most significant Urban Christian network.

He now operates multiple LIVE Shows that bring in thousands of views per week, including The Young Prophet, Young Preacher Movement, "When The Wrong One Comes". Men's Perspective. Davis' objective is to use his positive influence and global platform to impact
the lives of others.

PRODUCTS AND SERVICES

On Social Media the Search Handle : Greg Davis @bishopgregdavis

Facebook- Greg Davis @bishopgregdavis
Instagram - Greg Davis @bishopgregdavis
TikTok - Greg Davis @bishopgregdavis
Clubhouse Threads Bluesky - Greg Davis @bishopgregdavis

Watch ON YouTube
Channel: When The Right One Comes.

INQUIRIES
EMAIL: gregdavisshow@gmail.com OR gregdavis@gmail.com.

PRODUCTS
Website to purchase other products and books and set up counseling sessions.
www.gregdavisshow.com